KENNY BAKER

The Life and Times of a Jazz Musician

KENNY BAKER AND HIS LEGENDARY DOZEN
– all fifteen of them – return to centre stage at the
Birmingham International Jazz Festival, July 8th 1994.

KENNY BAKER

The Life and Times of a Jazz Musician

THE AUTHORISED
BIOGRAPHY BY

ROBERT G. CROSBY

WITH A FOREWORD BY
JACK PARNELL

EVERGREEN GRAPHICS
CRAIGWEIL ON SEA
ALDWICK

A Christmas card to grandma, 1937, from a proud 16 year-old bandsman, Kenny Baker.

KENNY BAKER
THE LIFE AND TIMES OF A JAZZ MUSICIAN

© R.G. Crosby 1999

First published in 1999 by
EverGreen Graphics
Kufri, 11 The Drive, Craigweil On Sea
Aldwick, West Sussex PO21 4DU

ISBN 1 900192 03 9

Designed by Cecil Smith
Typeset by EverGreen Graphics
Craigweil On Sea, Aldwick, West Sussex PO21 4DU

Printed and bound in the United Kingdom by
Redwood Books Ltd
Kennet Way, Trowbridge, Wiltshire BA14 8RN

Dedicated to
Prue
without whom
the book
would still
have been
at page 1.

No question as to who is the soloist. Kenny photographed during filming with the Eric Winstone Band and the Studio Strings.

CONTENTS

KENNY BAKER
starring in a Jack Parnell Band TV show.

ACKNOWLEDGEMENTS

NOT MANY BIOGRAPHERS have the enormous advantage of the full assistance of the subject of the biography, and my first thanks have to be to Kenny Baker, whose humour and astounding memory have made this book a pleasure to compile. It has also been an experience to meet up with what is described in the book as 'the League of Gentlemen' - namely Jack Parnell, Don Lusher, Roy Willox, Brian Lemon, and Lennie Bush, otherwise known as the Best Of British Jazz. Thanks are also due to various national publications for permission to use extracts from *The Melody Maker, New Musical Express, Sunday Pictorial, and Daily Express.* Jim Simpson of Big Bear Music has been one of many enthusiasts regarding the subject of the book, to which we must add the names of Mick Mulligan, Moira Heath, and Kath Jones of the Withernsea Lighthouse Trust. Closer to home thanks are due to Ron Gunner, Peggy Cox and proof reader Andrew Turner.

We have tried to acknowledge all the photographs and quotes in the book, but should there be any omissions, we will remedy this in future editions.

FOREWORD

by Jack Parnell

IT IS MY PLEASURE to get the chance to pay a tribute to someone I have known for over fifty years, and I am delighted to have the opportunity in a book which the world of swing music will welcome. The cliché is to say that he and I go back a long way, but in this case it is very true. We first met in 1943 when both of us were embarking on careers in the dance and swing bands, the music of which had crossed the Atlantic during World War Two. Since then our paths have intertwined and I am happy to know that our relationship has extended from that of mutually respected musicians to that of close friends.

Kenny brings to all who meet up with him, in live concerts or television studio, an amazing ebullience and joie de vivre which gets the best out of all of us. His trumpet technique can leave us (but not him) breathless, and whether jamming with him in a wartime night club, or swinging along with one of his many big band arrangements, we can only admire a man who is intrinsically modest until he picks up that horn.

I can only say that the nation should be proud of this Yorkshireman, who all his life has shown us that he is equally at home with the best international jazz musicians, or the brass bands that started him off in the distant past, in his home town of Withernsea.

It's been great playing along with you Kenny, and long may it continue!

Jack Parnell's Ode

I heard a trumpet years ago,
　A blast to bring down Jericho.
I hear that trumpet still today,
　So wondrous still in every way.
Long may his trumpet sounds ring out,
　Long may the audiences shout!

Jack Parnell.

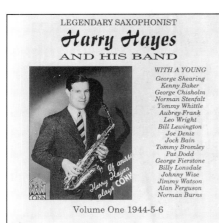

- SEQUENCE
- NEEDLE NOSE
- FIVE FLAT FLURRY
- FIRST EDITION
- DROP ME OFF IN HARLEM
- MERELY A MINOR
- 1/2/3/4 JUMP
- UP
- NO SCRIPT
- CHERRY BRANDY
- MIDNIGHT PROWL
- PLAYBOY
- HOMEWARD BOUND
- SWINGING ON LENNOX AVENUE
- KEEP GOING – DON'T STOP
- CAN'T YOU READ BETWEEN THE LINES

HARRY HAYES AND HIS BAND
VOLUME ONE 1944-5-6
Harry Hayes Musicals HH01CD

including
- LISTEN TO MY MUSIC
- TAIL END CHARLIE
- EAST OF THE SUN
- AD LIB FROLIC
- CHELSEA
- FINE ROMANCE
- DEEP NIGHT
- BABY BLUE
- ON WITH THE DON
- LULLABY OF BIRDLAND
- OPUS ONE
- OBSESSION
- HOT TODDY
- A DEDICATION TO MOIRA – SHEILA'S THEME
and many more

THE VERY BEST OF TED HEATH
VOLUME ONE
Horatio Nelson Records CDSIV 6150 1995

- HOW'S THIS
- LOVE ME OR LEAVE ME
- IF I COULD BE WITH YOU
- KEEPIN' OUT OF MISCHIEF NOW
- HOW CAN YOU FACE ME?
- PUTTIN' ON THE RITZ
- DOO-DEE
- ST. LOUIS BLUES
- HONOLULU BLUES
- MINUTE TO MIDNIGHT
- BLUES IN THIRDS
- APEX BLUES
- I'M A DING DONG DADDY
- STUDIO B BOOGIE
- WEST WIND
- OH, BABY

KENNY BAKER PRESENTS the half dozen … after hours
Lake Records LACD 88 1997 Original recordings 1955/57
Featuring George Chisholm, Dill Jones and
Bruce Turner in their hey day.

including
- LOVE, YOU FUNNY THING
- THE NEW TIGER RAG
- KEEPIN' OUT OF MISCHIEF NOW
- LAWD, YOU MADE THE NIGHT TOO LONG
- THAT'S MY HOME
- HOBO YOU CAN'T RIDE THIS TRAIN
- I HATE TO LEAVE YOU NOW
- HIGH SOCIETY
- BASIN STREET BLUES
- HONEY, DO!
- SNOWBALL
and many more

New Digital Recording Of The Authentic Musical
Biography Performed by KENNY BAKER
CD Vol. 7

including
- CARNIVAL TIME
- I CAN'T GET STARTED
- WON'T YOU COME HOME BILL BAILEY
- SATCHMO
- WHAT'S NEW
- LITTLE JAZZ
- SUGAR BLUES
- TENDERLY
- GEORGIA
- DAVENPORT BLUES
- MORNING GLORY
- ECHOES OF HARLEM
- MEMORIES OF YOU
and many more

KENNY BAKER & HIS ORCHESTRA
Tribute To The Great Trumpeters
Horatio Nelson Records CDSIV 1124 1993

- AFTER YOU'VE GONE
- AIN'T MISBEHAVIN'
- MOONLIGHT IN VERMONT
- WHO'S SORRY NOW
- LET'S CALL THE WHOLE THING OFF
- JUST A GIGOLO
- YOU STEPPED OUT OF A DREAM
- ROYAL GARDEN BLUES
- THESE FOOLISH THINGS
- I CAN'T GIVE YOU ANYTHING BUT LOVE, BABY
- STRIKE UP THE BAND
- WHEN YOU WISH UPON A STAR
- ROBBINS NEST
- BROADWAY

KENNY BAKER and WARRREN VACHÉ
AIN'T MISBEHAVIN'
Zephyr Records ZECD 17 1996/97

CHAPTER 1

THE BEST OF BRITISH JAZZ
The current band members talk about one of jazz's unique characters

"We are pleased to learn that Ken Baker, the Withernsea boy, has been successful in passing the BBC studio audition and he will broadcast from Leeds on March 3rd, at 8.45 to 9.30pm in 'Yorkshire Round-up'. Ken will play trumpet solos, and with his partner (Alf Young), accordion duets. Good luck Ken, and we won't forget to listen in." WITHERNSEA GAZETTE

S O HERALDED THE *Withernsea Gazette* in 1936 announcing the first broadcast of the fifteen year old Kenny who was to become one of Britain's finest trumpeters, whether featuring in the best post war bands – who can forget the Ted Heath brass section – or leading his own bands. He has been a performer since the age of 12, some 66 years at the time of writing. He has come a long way since his debut at the Queen's Hotel, in his local town of Withernsea, a small fishing and holiday centre near Hull. Even an enthusiastic local paper could not have anticipated that here was a young man who was to appear at Royal Command Performances, as well as accompanying American jazz musicians of the calibre of Billie Holiday and Benny Goodman on their visits to the UK. His music continues literally to hit the highest notes, and his popularity is not surprising to anyone

The original
'BEST OF BRITISH JAZZ'
playing at The Tram Shed,
Woolwich in 1980, (LtoR)
Don Lusher, Kenny Baker,
Betty Smith, Bill le Sage.
On drums Jack Parnell, on
bass Tony Archer.

who has had the privilege of meeting or working with one of Britain's great jazz personalities.

These days we are most likely to hear Kenny with the 'Best of British Jazz', a name which fairly reflects the quality of its members. For some twenty years he has been leading the group, a band which epitomises the man as well as the talent of the all star line up. The band started in an informal way in the early 70's when Kenny joined forces with tenor player Betty Smith, then playing with the Freddie Randall band. In addition he was able to attract Don Lusher on trombone, Tony Archer on bass, Tony Lee on piano, and Jack Parnell on drums. Although an impressive line-up there were problems. With no written routines, sometimes things got out of hand and matters came to a head when Betty had to give up with health problems. The band wound up, and it was some time before the new 'Best of British' jazz band was formed, and Kenny, Don and Jack decided that written arrangements were necessary.

"One thing is clear. There is only one Kenny Baker. His playing and writing, his great know-how of jazz and his strong personality, defines the man we know as K.B."

DON LUSHER (TROMBONE)

The new ensemble had Kenny on trumpet, Don on trombone, Roy Willox on tenor, and a strong rhythm section including Brian Lemon on piano, Lennie Bush on bass and of course Jack Parnell on drums. With this band they could arrive at the theatre, carry out a sound check, and then playing from Kenny's arrangements, produce a quality performance. The 'Best of British Jazz', as we know it today had arrived, and continues to the present.

One of the pleasures of working with Kenny on this book has been the opportunity to talk with many of his musical colleagues. It is difficult to meet a more lively bunch than the members of 'The Best of British' band. At a session during a 'tea' break in a concert at Chichester Festival Theatre, each was anxious to talk of their own experiences working with Kenny. It seemed a good idea to give each his head, so some idea of the man can be obtained from their remarks. Needless to say, each had a very high opinion of, and respect for, someone whom they had all known for up to fifty five years.

P&O ORIANA,
one of the cruise liners for which the current 'Best of British Jazz' is a welcome addition.

✫ DON LUSHER ✫

Like most of the band, Don Lusher has known Kenny for more years than he cares to remember. The first time he ever saw Kenny was while on army leave, when he and a friend queued for one and a half hours at the Hammersmith Palais to see the early Ted Heath band. Kenny was one of his heroes, and Don was amazed to see Kenny sweep by in an immaculate Crombie overcoat, 'looking like a film star'. They were to meet regularly in the future as both became leading performers in the jazz world. They still meet when playing with 'The Best of British Jazz', in Don's own Big Band or when Kenny is playing with the Ted Heath Band which continues under Don's baton. Through all this, Don says, 'One thing is clear. There is only one Kenny Baker. His playing and writing, his great know-how of jazz and his strong personality, defines the man we know as K.B'.

✫ JACK PARNELL ✫

As with the rest of this talented group, Jack Parnell has an amazing pedigree, first with his drumming for all the top bands, including his own, then when he chose a change in career in 1957 as Musical Director of ATV Television. 2,500 TV shows kept him busy until 1982, since then he came back to his love of drumming. All this time he kept in touch professionally and musically with Kenny who he first met in the early 40's. 'In my view, the irrepressible Kenny Baker is not only a great trumpet player, but the best DIY

expert I've ever come across. He can do anything, decorate, plumb, tile, garden, make wine, you name it! I remember going to a party at his house when he suddenly said "Come and listen to this". I thought he was going to play me some music, but he took me into the bathroom and flushed the toilet. "Listen to that, you can hardly hear it, perfectly balanced. All my own work !"

✫ BRIAN LEMON ✫

Regular winner of the Piano Section of the British Jazz Awards, Brian Lemon is one of the best known British pianists, and has played with just about everybody on the jazz scene. Always a pleasure to listen to, he has an enormous respect for Kenny.

'In my early teens I used to listen to Kenny on radio and records, never realising that one day I would actually play with him. There are no ordinary nights with Kenny – one is always aware of being in the presence of greatness. I always consider it an honour and privilege to be in his company both musically and socially.'

✫ LENNIE BUSH ✫

Lennie Bush has many happy memories of working with Kenny. 'In the late forties, I used to go to the Hammersmith Palais, as did many other musicians, to hear the Ted Heath Band and its leading light Kenny Baker; in the fifties I was a member of his original "Baker's Dozen"; and in the sixties Kenny and I were both in the Jack Parnell Band at ATV. Now in

the nineties I am with him in the 'The Best of British' and he is still an icon.

In all these years he has never failed to astound everyone with his playing – especially other trumpet players. I am always surprised by his energy and strength and confidence, and his ability to have 48 hours in each day. He is the only person I know who can pave a driveway, write a new band arrangement, and play a gig all in one day. After fifty years he still never fails to amaze me'.

✫ ROY WILLOX ✫

'Kenny is a legend in his own lifetime among the all-time great players world-wide. A wonderful lead player and a great interpreter of melody – he does a great "Louis, Bix or Harry James", yet his own style shows very little influence from any of his forbears.

In the TV studios he was usually engrossed in reading a magazine – not music, but DIY, cine photography and more recently camper vans. In recent years it has been a great pleasure to play alongside him in the Best of British Jazz. It never ceases to be fun, and a great musical treat.

Kenny Baker is truly the first and last of his kind'.

**The current
'BEST OF
BRITISH JAZZ'**

KENNY BAKER, trumpet / vocals
ROY WILLOX, reeds
BRIAN LEMON, piano
DON LUSHER, trombone
LENNIE BUSH, bass
JACK PARNELL, drums / vocals

The League of Gentlemen today.

The new band appointed Jack Higgins as manager, and often in a joint programme with Acker Bilk or Kenny Ball, the band continues to draw good audiences around the UK. There is always a demand for the beautiful trombone playing of Don Lusher, and Jack Parnell drives the band along with his drums, vocals and fund of jokes. The lyrical Roy Willox on sax and a superb rhythm section of Brian Lemon on piano with Lennie Bush on bass, means that we do have 'The Best of British'. To see them in action is to recognise that here is talent indeed, which coupled with enthusiasm and good leadership, reminds us continuously how lucky we have been to hear them through so many years. It is not surprising that Kenny feels in 1999 that he is still able to enjoy his music, and in particular can still astound the audience with the quality and power of his trumpet playing.

But how did it all start ?

CHAPTER 2

THE EARLY DAYS
Withernsea sea front to the West End

Iᴛ ᴡᴀꜱ ǫᴜɪᴛᴇ ᴀ ʟᴀʀɢᴇ ꜱᴛᴇᴘ from the bandstand at the small fishing and holiday village of Withernsea, near Hull, to the stage of Royal Command Performances in London, but from his youngest days, Kenny showed the talent and determination to do just that. His parents had emigrated from the boot and shoe centres of Northamptonshire to Withernsea near Hull, where Kenny was born on March 1st, 1921.

Both his mother and father were excellent boot and shoe makers – handmade in those days. This business continued to keep house and home together, but music was very much part of family life. Mother was an accomplished musician, playing piano, violin, and accordion; Dad indulged himself with the saxophone, and both of them played in a variety of dance-bands at a time when dancing was the normal leisure activity, in particular for the young. They also entertained by singing humourous duets, and this

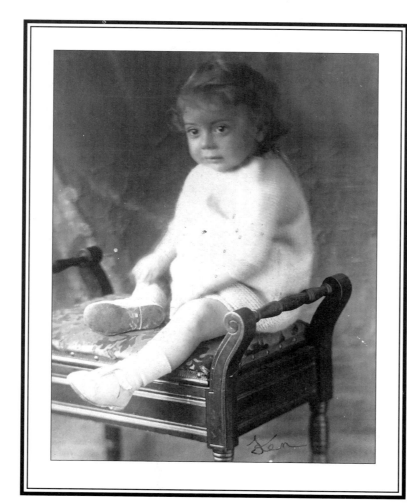

A thoughtful Kenny aged two. The piano stool was to be more significant than anyone suspected in 1923.

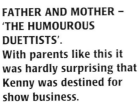

**FATHER AND MOTHER –
'THE HUMOUROUS
DUETTISTS'.**
**With parents like this it
was hardly surprising that
Kenny was destined for
show business.**

**The 'cheekie chappie'
in borrowed hat and
gloves,aged five.**

was all in addition to earning a living in the shoe trade, and raising a family. The young Kenny often accompanied his parents to the evening dances and concerts, and remembers being taken home on father's back at midnight.

He went to an elementary school in Withernsea – although it was a good school, Kenny seemed more interested in music than in academic studies. This was hardly surprising in a home where he could get back for tea only to be told by his father that "there's no tea yet, mum's upstairs practicing the piano". As well as working and bringing up a family, she received four musical qualifications, one for piano, one for accordion, one for singing, and one for the violin.

It was also the time of silent films, and such was his mother's talent that she was invited to form a small orchestra to accompany the films in the local cinemas. The band was quite small, piano, violin, cello, bass and drums. Kenny's mother would watch the screen and having chosen the appropriate music, would lead the orchestra playing music to suit the action. Each musician had his or her own set of fifty or more pieces, and at a signal from the leader, struck up the sad or exciting tune which was vital in not ruining the love scenes of Rudolph Valentino or the antics of Charlie Chaplin. She recalled the mad flurry of papers as the tempo of the film changed, and she and her orchestra changed from 'one minute heavy' to 'one minute light'. 'Music was just thrown to the floor in the changeover. Then before the second house we had to collect it and sort it out to begin again'. For this she earned a comfortable £4.10s a week. It was hardly surprising that her son was moving steadily into the world of professional music making. Kenny said that he used to go nearly every night, and saw

such films as *Felix the Cat* and the original *Ben Hur* at least six times.

KENNY'S MOTHER (middle, seated) with one of her two accordion bands.

Kenny's uncle was a tuba player in the Gospel Mission band which could be found most weekends on Withernsea sea front. This was a collection of individuals who played in the street to raise money for charity, and for eleven year old Kenny it meant the chance to play the tenor horn, then the cornet, both of which he took to readily. The fact that he really wanted to take up the tuba was ignored, for which we can be grateful. Like some other *ad hoc* groups, at an appropriate point, the organiser absconded with the takings!

His early lessons with his mother meant that he was familiar with music theory and harmony, and had the ability to read music. These together with his early piano accordion lessons, were to stand him in good stead for what was to become a brilliant musical future.

**THE GOSPEL MISSION
BAND OF WITHERNSEA
– unfortunately the
profits disappeared with
the organiser.
Kenny bottom right.**

An interesting insight into life at the time is reflected in a letter to the 'Old Codgers' in the *Daily Mirror* in January 1968. The letter speaks for itself, and paints a picture of a happy household in prewar days.

When his parents moved to Hull, he was given the choice of moving with them and continuing his school studies, or staying on in Withernsea with his sister 'provided you practice most of the day'. He chose the latter, but still preferred football to working at his scales. It certainly saw the end of his academic schooling

He eventually decided to join his parents in Hull, and was accepted into the West Hull Silver Prize Excelsior Brass Band at the age of fourteen , where he soon excelled on the cornet. The young Kenny was soon to be soloist of that prestigious band. It was around this time when he acquired his first trumpet, complete with case, mouthpiece and mute, all for five pounds!

So at the age of around fifteen he was competent on trumpet, cornet and accordion, and with his friend Alf Young (accordion and piano) he formed a duo which went round the hotels earning money with a performance which included accordion duets, trumpet solos and all four combinations of the four instruments. His first gig earned him two half crowns, one of which his mother gave back to him. And he still has it !

CONDUCTED BY THE OLD CODGERS
LETTERS

In the depths of winter most people's minds turn to thoughts of holidays. JACK BUCK, of Gravesend, Kent, writes to us about boyhood holidays spent with a remarkable family:

READING about cinema pianists in the days of silent films brought to mind a wonderful character, Mrs. Baker, who kept a boarding house at Withernsea, Yorkshire.

As a youngster I, with my family, spent very many happy summers with Mrs. Baker. She would cook, serve, laugh and entertain her guests on violin, piano, and in song, between and after her matinee and evening performances at "The Pictures."

Her husband was also a musician, more by enthusiasm than ability, and he played in a band at the local dance hall and skating rink. I was there when his first saxophone was delivered by the postman. The smile on his and Mrs. Baker's face when they unpacked it and he blew the first notes, trilling up and down the scales, was music at its best.

The Bakers' front room was a wonderful shop, selling pinafores, papers, pins, pants and penny-whistles. Mr. Baker also repaired boots and had a big gas engine to drive polishing and buffing wheels. The sound of that engine and the smells of leather, polish and oil were childhood joys I still remember.

He had an old bull-nosed Morris and he would take us children round the villages and along the narrow Spurn Point to the lighthouse, delivering papers and selling needles, cotton dresses and shoes. We preferred those trips to building sand castles or paddling!

The Bakers had a daughter and a small boy. He was below school age then, but he could already play the Jew's harp, mouth-organ, piano, violin, piccolo—and a tin trumpet. He obviously liked the trumpet best and I believe he must now be the famous jazz trumpeter, Kenny Baker.

☆ We spoke to Kenny about your letter and he was obviously moved. He said: "That's me, all right. I'm sorry to say my parents are now dead, but it certainly brings my childhood back."

And happy characters like that never really die, do they?

● THE OLD CODGERS' address is "Live Letters," Daily Mirror, 33, Holborn, London, E.C.1.

'THE OLD CODGERS COLUMN'
in the 'Daily Mirror'
January 1968.

WEST HULL SILVER PRIZE BRASS BAND.
The smallest, the youngest, the cornet soloist Kenny Baker, back row, far left.

Lead cornet aged 16 showed
the way things were going –
at 23 he was to be lead
trumpet player with the
Ted Heath Orchestra.

When he was fifteen he and partner Alf were invited to play in a BBC radio programme in Leeds called *Yorkshire Round-up*, and this was his first broadcast. His radio appearances had started, and he now had to decide just in which direction his talents were to take him.

That summer he parted from Alf to join a band playing a season at Great Yarmouth, while back home in Hull he worked with some of the best bands and formed his own combo. His mother had given him a good academic training, and fully expected him to become a classical musician. However a local drummer asked him round one day to listen to some of his records of Duke Ellington and Louis Armstrong.

That changed everything!

CHARLOTTE BAKER, an attractive mother who could lay down the law when it came to Kenny's accordion and cornet practice.

A faded, but atmospheric photo of music for dancing – Kenny's father far left, and mother in front of drums.

**BROADCASTING DUO,
KENNY BAKER AND
ALF YOUNG.**
The local paper reported,
'We are pleased that Kenny
Baker, the Withernsea boy,
has been successful in
passing the BBC audition
and he will broadcast from
Leeds on March 3rd, in
'Yorkshire Round-Up.'
Ken will play trumpet
solos, and with his partner
Alf Young, accordion.
Good luck, Ken, and we
won't forget to listen in.'

**QUEEN'S HOTEL,
WITHERNSEA**
Where Kenny played
some of his earliest gigs.

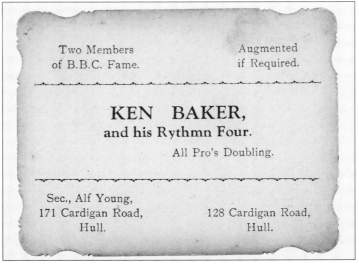

This card could book
the 16 year old and his
Rhythm Four, two members
of BBC fame'!

CHAPTER 3

KING AND COUNTRY
Aircrafthand Baker, the RAF's secret weapon

HAVING HEARD his first recordings of American jazz, Kenny set about learning more about this new music. He was so taken with this that he joined a dance band where he could learn about the new music and more importantly, he started to make arrangements, using his self taught arranging techniques. He was soon completely sold on the big band scene which was to feature so strongly in his career, and he was making money!

Work in Hull was limited, and he answered an advertisement to join Sandy Powell who was touring in variety. The 18 year old Kenny remembers the act before his, which consisted of father and son who were acrobats - they finished their act with the son balanced upside down on father's head, while they played a cornet duet. Follow that! At a later date, Sandy's musical director asked him to join Sandy in London, and Kenny accepted. This was an important decision because it brought him to the West End of London, where anything could happen. Things were fine for two weeks, then the show closed, as did a lot of the West End theatres at the beginning of the War. Out of work with very little money, (mother always advised him to keep his train fare home), Kenny frequented Archer Street, that famous street where musicians congregated looking for work. Luckily, he landed a job at the Streatham Locarno – at £5 a week. 'We're in the money!' While at the Locarno, Kenny was to meet pianist Norman Stenfalt, with whom he was to work for many happy years.

1394960 Leading Aircraftman
Baker K. 1941-1946.

He started at the Locarno on the Monday ,and on the Wednesday while in Archer Street he was told that Lew Stone was looking for a trumpet player. The show was *Keep it under your Hat* and featured Cicely Courtnedge and Jack Hulbert at the Palace Theatre. At an audition Lew said 'I'll give you a two week trial if you can start next Monday'. Kenny left the Locarno and joined Lew for £8.8.0. a week. 'We're in the more money'!

At the end of two weeks Kenny waited at the stage door to see whether he had really got the job. Lew swept by with a curt 'Good-night' to the doorman, ignoring the anxious Kenny who didn't know what to do next. The doorman said : 'If I were you I would turn up on Monday'. Kenny did, and stayed until the show closed.

Since working with Lew Stone, with men joining the armed forces daily, the eighteen old Kenny found himself working with a variety of the country's leading bands, including Ambrose, Jack Hylton, Geraldo and Maurice Winnick. His talent was certainly up to it, but he was still fortunate at this young age to get experience with such an illustrious collection of the country's top bands.

Hardly the ballroom at the Mayfair Hotel with Ambrose, rather a muddy field at RAF Bentley Priory, Stanmore with Warrant Officer Wheeler in charge of the band. Kenny back row, second from right.

By now he was becoming well known in the business, and was deputising for other trumpeters of the day who needed a stand-in. He first met Ambrose when deputising for trumpeter Chick Smith, when the band was playing at the Mayfair Hotel. A nervous Kenny was advised 'Just walk in, ask for Ambrose, you'll be OK.' He was, and enjoyed playing with the top dance band of the day in one of the most prestigious venues. The only problem was that no-one had mentioned money, so again a nervous Kenny called on Ambrose a few days later, and asked for his fee. 'How much do you want' the leader asked, and then without waiting for a reply, pulled out the largest roll of money Kenny had ever seen, and peeled off £3. Kenny had made it with the best, and always had a soft spot for Ambrose, lasting many years. Although not a regular member of the band, Kenny was on most of the Ambrose recordings made in the early 40's.

The latter's gambling sometimes caused concern with the band, and in France he managed to lose all his cash and his Rolls Royce in a bout of gambling. The band's money was despatched from London, and all relaxed. Ambrose made huge sums when in his heyday, but was to lose it all.

For the young Kenny, the Ambrose band introduced him to another world. Many engagements were in the most luxurious hotels in London, and this was probably the only band to receive a telegram while in New York saying :

'THE EMBASSY NEEDS YOU STOP COME BACK STOP EDWARD P'.

The embassy referred to was the Embassy Club in London, and the sender was the Duke of Windsor! Ambrose obeyed the command and the band returned to London. Kenny recounts the story of King Alphonse of Spain and the Duke of Windsor asking to sit in on drums and bass. Ambrose was on violin and they were joined by Ambrose's pianist. To a rich dowager's comments that 'You have a lovely little band Mr Ambrose', he replied 'Perhaps so my lady, but you wouldn't be able to afford them'. Those were the days!

Further experience with such as Ambrose, Jack Hylton and the Sid Milward Big Band, and all night sessions at the 400 Club, ensured him a good living as well as preparing him for what was to come. Life with the country's best bands, and a flat off Leicester Square, meant that at the age of eighteen Kenny was able to enjoy the bright lights of what was still reckoned to be the world's greatest city.

Unfortunately Adolf Hitler was to change all that, and on the declaration of war in 1939, one of the first things that happened was the closing of most of London's theatres as the Government took stock. At the same time, night clubs were closed, one reason being given that the nation's secrets could have been given away by drunken Britishers consorting with the many beautiful German spies that were assumed to be in the country.

A matter of some relief to Kenny was his inability to accept an offer to play with the Ken 'Snake Hips' Johnson band in London's Café de Paris, a popular night club in the heart of London. Kenny had been asked to join the Café de Paris band, but he was already committed to the Jack Hylton

There was a war on, as this bizarre band picture confirms !

show which was touring the country. The show was called *Garrison Theatre* with Jack Warner, and included a stage band fronted by Sid Milward. Kenny joined the show which was touring Moss Empire theatres.

While on tour he heard that a German bomb had fallen down the ventilation shaft of the Café de Paris, and tragically the leader Ken Johnson was killed and guitarist Joe Deniz injured, as well as several members of the public. This was a near miss for Kenny, who later in his career was to join the re-formed band, when it was taken over by reed player Carl Baritteau.

With the nation at war, Kenny was well aware that serving his king and country was likely. Army food and the possibility of joining the infantry did not appeal to him, so volunteering to become one of the 'Brylcreem Boys' seemed a more attractive alternative, and he saw a future for himself in the RAF. He also realised that one danger in the Services lies in volunteering for anything. It could well be that a volunteer trumpet player is likely to be posted as a cook or rear gunner on a four engined bomber. Not wishing to be in the cook-house or a hero, Kenny was lucky in knowing trombonist Harry Roche who had been in the forces before, and who seemed to know everyone in the field of RAF recruitment. He also knew that there were plans to set up a military band associated with Fighter Command. 'Put your name down' was his advice, happily taken and in 1942 Kenny found himself in Uxbridge, in Air Force blue, and in the company of quite a few of the West End's professional musicians.

The mace bearer on the left was Corporal Steve Race with the station band.

Hendon aerodrome was to be the base for the new band as it was being formed, and was to be Kenny's home intermittently for the early part of the war. As with most Service bandsmen, the discipline of the parade ground was replaced by the insistence on the ability to play any style of music. This meant military marches, light concert items, the classical repertoire and of course, to be one of the necessary eight brass, five saxes and rhythm section which constituted a swing band for dancing. The fact that he had been rigorously brought up with the idea that if you could handle 'the dots' you should always be able to get work, was confirmed by his service with the RAF Fighter Command Band. Wartime service kept Kenny on top of his trumpet skills as well as extending his considerable ability as arranger.

One of his first musical directors was Warrant Officer John Gardner, a man of many talents. 'We were rehearsing some boring, nondescript light orchestral piece and he happened to say "this is a load of rubbish – anyone could write stuff like this". Harry Roche the trombone player said "Well, why don't you"? Next morning John turned up with a new full score of 'Rustic Overture', with all parts written out, which we thought was very good. We played it that morning, after which he tore it up! This talented

The RAF introduce 'Aircrafthand / musician' bands for work on RAF stations and occasionally near the front line.

musician then remustered as air crew, and became a navigator. It was our loss.'

In his early days with the RAF he continued to be based at Hendon, and had the best of both worlds by having a 'sleeping out' pass which enabled him to have a flat in the West End. He was temporarily stationed at RAF

THE SQUADRONNAIRES
was an enormously popular
RAF dance band which
survived the war.
Kenny back row far right.
The occasion was the
opening of the London Stage
Door Canteen, attended by
Bing Crosby and Fred Astaire.

Duxford while the Fighter Command band was being formed. The procedure was to be 'on parade' at 8am, and by midday, you were free to do your own thing. He could thus play with the RAF in the daytime, and in various theatre and club bands in the evenings. He often did not get much sleep, but his evening gigs augmented his somewhat humble Service pay, and for a time he had a comfortable lifestyle. The new director Warrant Officer Parsons was originally unaware of the departure of most of his band to the West End after lunch. When he found that he couldn't have an afternoon meeting he insisted that they report to his office the next morning. 'We expected a terrible row, and were berated for leaving camp without permission. "You will not do this again". He then gave us a book of stamped, signed, but undated passes. What a lovely man!'

This phoney war syndrome was to be shattered when the band was to travel across liberated Europe, entertaining Allied servicemen who were fighting their way across France, Holland and Germany.

With America in the war, some of the finest American musicians were drafted into the forces, and although some finished up in the infantry or

1942. Back stage at the Palace Theatre,
Shaftesbury Avenue, Bobby Midgley on drums,
and Kenny, taking time off from the war.

(left)
1943. The mix of civilians and service personnel kept up the standards of big band performance, and at the same time kept the service musicians in touch with civvy street. This is the Frank Weir band, Kenny without uniform, back row second from left.

(bottom left)
EMI Studios 1941, recording a jazz session featuring Buddy Featherstonhaugh (tenor), Kenny (trumpet), Lad Busby (trombone), Carl Barriteau (clarinet).

(right)
HMV's first public 'jam session', Leslie 'Jiver' Hutchinson on right.

PHOTO J. HOLLANDER

similar fighting posts in the Army and Navy, many donned uniform and continued playing for such leaders as Artie Shaw, Glenn Miller and Sam Donahue. Prior to D-Day, Britain was packed with US military personnel and Kenny was able to listen to and play with various US military bands. After formal concerts, many musicians went along to the Nuthouse Club in the West End where American and British musicians shared the drinks and the sitting in on groups playing jazz for fun. Not many people can claim to have learnt 'How High the Moon' from Mel Powell, but this was the sort of opportunity that Kenny was happy to take up at one of these informal sessions, and able to build on later, as a key member of the future Ted Heath Orchestra. Meanwhile the troops were entertained to the best music of the day, and began to hear the Squadronnaires, the Fighter Command Band, and an American band based in Park Lane where Kenny was able to enjoy American standards of Army life. During this time he met such famous American musicians as Peanuts Hucko, Ray McKinley, and Glenn Miller.

A memorable visit was made after the liberation of Norway, when the Fighter Command band was sent to play in Oslo, at the various march pasts and ceremonies to welcome back King Haakon. The king had spent most of the war in the UK. German troops were still hiding in the Norwegian mountains and food generally was in desperately short supply. Kenny was one of the band not permitted to have a night out in the city, and was detailed to be one of a small band to play in the Officers' Mess. Although the 'volunteers' were not too happy about this, the evening turned out to be 'one of the best nights of my life'. The camp turned out to be adjoining the German Officers' mess, and an Aladdin's cave of food, wine and particularly champagne was found. A grateful acceptance of a British major's offer of a drink resulted in a bottle of the best champagne for each member of the band. By

PHOTO J. HOLLANDER

RAF BENEVOLENT CONCERT AT THE STATE CINEMA, KILBURN, 1942.
Kenny taking solo. This was the Ken Johnson Band whose leader sadly had been killed, due to a direct hit on the Café de Paris. Fortunately Kenny couldn't make the gig, although he had been asked. Joe Deniz (guitar) was injured, but made a full recovery.

THE FELDMAN CLUB, LONDON, 1941.
Foreground,
Robert Feldman (clarinet),
Monty Feldman (accordion);
just visible, the real talent in this musical family, the ten year old Victor Feldman (drums). Kenny back row, right.

midnight there were twenty empty bottles on the band stand, and many more full ones lined up. The next morning the band observed a truck carrying twenty more bottles of champagne, and the drummer said 'we might as well have them as well.' They returned to the UK, smuggling in the remainder of the champagne by removing the skins of the drummer's timpani,

inserting the bottles wrapped in Army blankets, replacing the skins and walking calmly, if unsteadily, past the authorities in Harwich docks.

The ten year old Victor Feldman, already an astounding drummer, and at the beginning of a career which took him to live in the USA. Our loss.

As the war approached its end, Kenny was transferred ('perhaps I had done something wrong') to the band of the RAF Regiment, where for the first time he was issued with a rifle. At this point, the Germans surrendered!

With the end of the war in Europe, Kenny was anxious to get back to the West End, and apart from involvement with 'Overseas Recording Broadcasts' for restricted use for the Armed Forces, he was remaking contacts with Civvy Street. Demob was easy if you could persuade the RAF that you had a job to go to, and this was no problem for a man of Kenny's talents. Ted Heath had started to form his new band, and Toots Camerata who had played with the Jimmy Dorsey Orchestra, had come over to England to direct music for a new film, *London Town*, with the very young Petula Clark and Sid Field. He needed a big swinging band, so he signed up the Ted Heath musicians. Kenny was one of these, and because he had a job to go to, was able to get his demob suit. Film-making was tedious, but gave them good contacts and a steady income for several weeks.

With his many contacts and with the back-up of the Archer Street 'job centre', he was always busy, and was soon playing with the Geraldo and Jack Jackson bands.

The way into these bands continued to be by deputising for other trumpet players who wanted time off, and this meant turning up at a gig, and reading the music cold. Arrangements were often on small cards, with a brief note – 'you solo here for eight bars'. It was nothing to play in a band for the evening, and during the intermission, to jump in a taxi and spend an hour in a recording studio, rushing back to catch the second half of the gig.

Fame brought its rewards − one of many advertisements before the days of TV advertising.

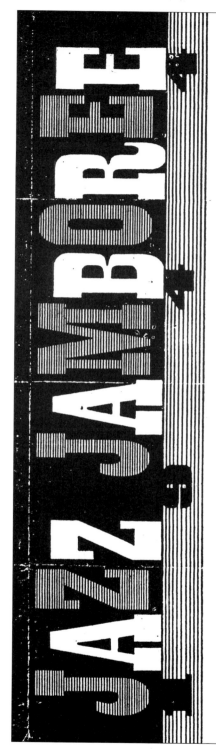

THE MUSICIANS'
SOCIAL AND BENEVOLENT COUNCIL

HAS PLEASURE IN PRESENTING

" JAZZ JAMBOREE, 1944 "

Dedicated to ALFRED H. MORGAN, the Council's
retiring Hon. Acting Secretary

STOLL THEATRE, KINGSWAY
SUNDAY, OCTOBER 15th, 1944

ACKNOWLEDGMENTS

The Council desire to express their gratitude to :—

The Stoll Picture Theatre (Kingsway), Ltd., and Staff for
their cordial co-operation.

The B.B.C. for broadcasting twenty-five minutes in the General
Forces Programme.

Tommy Trinder, for his co-operation and invaluable services
as Compère.

Every Band Leader, Vocalist, and Instrumentalist appearing in
the Bill.

The Entrants, Judges, Geraldo's Orchestra, The Dance
Orchestra of ·H.M. Royal Air Force, and all who have
contributed to the success of " Jazz Jamboree Award."

Every Band Leader, Compère, Vocalist, and Instrumentalist
who offered their services, but who, owing to length of
Programme, could not be accommodated.

All the Advertisers in the Programme who have so generously
taken space to help the Fund.

All the Voluntary Helpers in the Front and Back of the House;
the Stewards, Programme Sellers, and others.

Mr. Leon Goodman of Leon Goodman Displays, Ltd., for
designing the original Programme cover.

Messrs. Boosey & Hawkes for their kindness in supplying us
with Basses for use at this Concert.

Messrs. Chappell & Co., Ltd., for supplying their excellent
Grand Pianos.

The Premier Drum Co., Ltd., for supplying all Drum Outfits
for use at this Concert.

The *Melody Maker* and General Press for the help they have
given.

The London District Committee of the Musicians' Union for
permitting its members to appear gratuitously.

The Performing Right Society has granted free permission for
the use of its repertoire on this occasion and the Council
desire to thank the composers and owners of the copy-
right in the music performed for their generosity in
forgoing the fees to which they are entitled.

THE MUSICIANS' SOCIAL AND BENEVOLENT COUNCIL

5 Egmont House

116 Shaftesbury Avenue, London, W.1

Telephone : GERrard 6096

*This Programme is printed in accordance with
Wartime Regulations*

Price ONE SHILLING

PROGRAMME FOR JAZZ JAMBOREE CONCERT 1944,

'printed in accordance with Wartime Regulations'.
See pages 26/27 for amazing cast list.

PROGRAMME   Compere TOMMY TRINDER

THE LONDON COLISEUM ORCHESTRA
Under the Direction of REGINALD BURSTON

Violins :	JOE DEMBINA (Leader)	'Cellos :	J. BRADY
	M. JEKEL		J. SIGALL
	S. WALLER	Trumpets:	G. REGAN
	C. M. KEMP		G. MORGAN
	J. PALMER	Piano :	F. BRETON
	E. W. ANDERSON	Trombones :	D. CARTER
	W. PENMAN		E. SOWDEN
	H. CHEVERIN	Harp :	MAY SALKELD
Violas :	L. MEER	Drums & Tymps. :	WAG. ABBEY
	F. CRAMER	Flute & Piccolo :	R. E. CROSS
Clarinets :	A. BUTTEN	Bass :	W. MACDONALD
	J. CLEVERLEY		

LOU PREAGER AND HIS ORCHESTRA

1st Trumpet :	A. " TICH " CHARLTON	3rd Tenor Sax :	DENNIS CRACKNELL
2nd Trumpet :	HARRY FINCH	Baritone Sax :	FRED CRANSTONE
3rd Trumpet :	KEN EXTON	Guitar :	PAUL RICH
1st Alto & Clar. :	JACK CARTER	Bass :	DOUG. CALDERWOOD
2nd Alto :	DON PEARSALL	Drums :	NORRIS GRUNDY
1st Tenor Sax :	JOHNNIE GRAY	Piano :	BILLY PENROSE
2nd Tenor Sax :	NORMAN BURGESS	Vocaliste :	EDNA KAYE

FRANK DENIZ " SPIRITS OF RHYTHM "
(By arrangement with Eric Winstone)

Piano :	CLARE DENIZ	Electric Guitar :	FRANK DENIZ
Tenor Sax :	J. SKIDMORE	Bass :	T. WADMORE
Drums :	T. BUTLIN		

No. I BALLOON CENTRE DANCE ORCHESTRA
A Band of H.M. Royal Air Force
(By kind permission of the Officer Commanding)
Directed by PAUL FENOULHET

1st Trumpet :	CHICK SMITH	1st Tenor Sax :	CLIFF TIMMS
2nd Trumpet :	LES LAMBERT	2nd Tenor Sax :	BASIL SKINNER
3rd Trumpet :	TED ALLABY	Piano :	PAT DODD
1st Trombone :	HARRY ROCHE	Guitar :	JOE YOUNG
2nd Trombone :	JOE CORDELL	Bass :	JOCK REID
1st Alto Sax :	IZZY DUMAN	Drums :	GEORGE FIERSTONE
2nd Alto Sax :	BILL APPS	Vocalist :	DENNY DENNIS

THE FELDMAN TRIO
Clar. : ROBERT FELDMAN.   Piano-Acc. : MONTY FELDMAN.   Drums : VICTOR FELDMAN.

TED HEATH AND HIS MUSIC

Saxophones :	LESLIE GILBERT	Trombones :	TED HEATH
	MICHAEL KREIN		WOOLF PHILLIPS
	DEREK HAWKINS		LES CAREW
	AUBREY FRANKS		GEORGE ROWE
	NORMAN IMPEY	Drums :	JACK PARNELL
Trumpets :	MAX GOLDBERG	Piano :	RONNIE SELBY
	ARTHUR MOUNCEY	Guitar :	FREDDY PHILLIPS
	CLIFF HAINES	Bass :	GEORGE GARNETT
	RONNIE PRIEST		

ROBERTO INGLEZ AND HIS RUMBA BAND

Piano :	ROBERTO INGLEZ	Bass :	BILL WILDER
Bongoes :	BILLY DUFFY	Claves :	JAMES CUMMINGS
Guitar :	SID BISSETT	Maraccas :	LOUIS ORTIZ
Trumpet :	ANDREW COOK	Guiro :	DONALDO GRIFFITHS

"JAZZ JAMBOREE AWARD"
(A Competition for the Best Original Jazz Composition)
The Three Selected Entries for Final Judging
Judges : STANLEY BLACK, STANLEY BOWSHER, GEORGE EVANS, T/Sgt. JERRY GRAY, and
HARRY SARTON
Played by THE DANCE ORCHESTRA OF H.M. ROYAL AIR FORCE

FRANK WEIR AND HIS ORCHESTRA

Trumpets :	KENNY BAKER	Violins :	REG LEOPOLD
	ALFIE NOAKES		SID SAX
	TOMMY BALDERSON		CHARLES KATZ
Trombones :	LAD BUSBY		BILLY MILLER
	HARRY ROCHE	Violas :	CYRIL STAPLETON
	JIMMY COOMBS		MAURICE LOBAN
Saxophones :	CLIFF TOWNSHEND		DAVID BELLMAN
	HARRY SMITH	'Cellos :	MAURICE WESTERBY
	HARRY LEWIS		GEORGE ROTH
	FREDDY GARDNER	Drums :	NORMAN BURNS
	FRED BALLERINI	Bass :	DON STUTELY
		Guitar :	SID JACOBSON
		Piano :	GEORGE SHEARING

Where were you in 1944?

A list of musicians, British and American, including
some names already famous, and some yet to
make their names. L.A.C. Kenny Baker appears in
three of the bands !

GERALDO AND HIS ORCHESTRA

1st Trumpet :	ALFIE NOAKES	1st Tenor Sax :	BILLY AMSTELL
2nd Trumpet :	TIM CASEY	2nd Tenor Sax :	GEORGE HARRIS
3rd Trumpet :	CHICK SMITH	Baritone Sax :	PHIL GOODY
1st Trombone :	TED HEATH	Piano :	SIDNEY BRIGHT
2nd Trombone :	ERIC TANN	Drums :	MAURICE BURMAN
3rd Trombone :	JOE FERRIE	Guitar :	IVOR MAIRANTS
1st Alto Sax :	DOUGIE ROBINSON	Bass :	JACK COLLIER
2nd Alto Sax :	WALLY STOTT	Vocalists :	LEN CAMBER
			JOHNNY GREEN

PHIL GREEN AND HIS DIXIELAND BAND

Trumpet :	DUNCAN WHYTE	Drums :	JOHNNY MARKS
Trombone :	JOCK BAIN	Bass :	MAURICE REID
Clarinet :	DAVE GREEN	Guitar :	DENNIS WRIGHT
Tenor Sax :	ARTY WILLIAMS	Piano :	MARION LOTHIAN

THE DANCE ORCHESTRA OF H.M. ROYAL AIR FORCE
(By kind permission of the Air Council)

Vocalist (Cond'or) :	Sgt. JIMMY MILLER	Saxophones :	L.A.C. TOMMY BRADBURY
Trumpets :	Cpl. TOMMY McQUATER		L.A.C. MONTY LESTER
	L.A.C. ARCHIE CRAIG		L.A.C. ANDY McDEVITT
	L.A.C. KENNY BAKER		L.A.C. JIMMY DURRANT
Trombones :	L.A.C. ERIC BREEZE	Guitar :	L.A.C. SID COLIN
	L.A.C. GEORGE CHISHOLM	Bass :	L.A.C. ARTHUR MADEN
Piano :	L.A.C. RONNIE ALDRICH	Drums :	L.A.C. JOCK CUMMINGS

VIC LEWIS–JACK PARNELL AND THEIR JAZZMEN

Guitar :	VIC LEWIS	Clarinet :	CLIFF TOWNSHEND
Drums :	JACK PARNELL	Piano :	DICK KATZ
Trumpet :	BILLY RIDDICK	Bass :	BERT HOWARD
Sop. & Alto Sax :	RONNY CHAMBERLAIN		

ALL-STAR BAND ("MELODY MAKER" POLL 1944)

Trumpets :	KENNY BAKER	Alto Saxes :	HARRY HAYES
	TOMMY McQUATER		DOUGIE ROBINSON
	CHICK SMITH	Tenor Saxes :	AUBREY FRANKS
	ARTHUR MOUNCEY		BUDDY
Trombones :	GEORGE CHISHOLM		FEATHERSTONHAUGH
	(Leader)	Baritone Sax :	JIMMY DURRANT
	WOOLF PHILLIPS	Piano :	GEORGE SHEARING
	ERIC BREEZE	Drums :	JACK PARNELL
	DON MACAFFER	Guitar :	IVOR MAIRANTS
		Bass :	TOMMY BROMLEY

THE AMERICAN BAND OF THE A.E.F.
Conducted by MAJOR GLENN MILLER

Executive Officer :	Lt. DON W. HAYNES	Director of Programmes :	W.O. PAUL DUDLEY
Piano :	S/Sgt. MEL POWELL	French Horn :	Cpl. ADDISON COLLINS, Jr.
	Cpl. JACK RUSIN	Violins :	S/Sgt. GEORGE OCKNER
Drums :	T/Sgt. RAY McKINLEY		S/Sgt. HARRY KATZMAN
	Cpl. FRANK IPPOLITO		Cpl. ERNEST KARDOS
Guitar :	Sgt. CARMEN MASTREN		Cpl. EUGENE BERGEN
Bass :	S/Sgt. TRIGGER ALPERT		S/Sgt. CARL SWANSON
	Cpl. JOE SHULMAN		Cpl. MILTON EDELSON
Trumpets :	M/Sgt. ZEKE ZARCHY		Sgt. DAVE HERMAN
	Sgt. BOB NICHOLS		Cpl. PHIL COGLIANO
	Sgt. WHITEY THOMAS		Cpl. JOSEPH KOWALEWSKI
	Sgt. BERNIE PRIVEN		Sgt. DAVE SCHWARTZ
	Cpl. JACK STEELE		Cpl. HENRY BRYNAN
Trombones :	Sgt. JIMMY PRIDDY		Cpl. EARL CORNWELL
	Cpl. JOHN HALLIBURTON		P.F.C. FRED OSTROVSKY
	Cpl. LARRY HALL		Cpl. MORRIS BIALKIN
	P.F.C. NAT PECK		Cpl. BOB RIPLEY
Vocalist :	Sgt. JOHNNIE DESMOND		Cpl. STANLEY HARRIS
Crew Chiefs :	Sgt. STEVE STECK		Cpl. EMANUEL WISHNOW
	Cpl. EUGENE STECK		Cpl. DAVE SACKSON
	Cpl. ARTHUR MALVIN		Cpl. NATE KAPROFF
	Cpl. MURRAY KANE		Cpl. RICHARD
	Cpl. LYNN ALLISON		MOTOLINSKI
Saxophones :	S/Sgt. HANK FREEMAN	Arrangers :	T/Sgt. JERRY GRAY
	Sgt. MICHAEL HUCKO		M/Sgt. NORM LAYDEN
	Sgt. VINCE CARBONE		S/Sgt. RALPH WILKINSON
	Sgt. JACK FERRIER		S/Sgt. JIMMY JACKSON
	Cpl. FRED GUERRA		
	Cpl. MANN THALER		

Production : T/Sgt. GEORGE VOUTSAS & Sgt. HARRY HARTWICK

Stage Manager : Sgt. JULIUS ZIFFERBLATT

Announcer : Cpl. PAUL DUBOV

Asst. Executive Officers : T/Sgt. JACK SANDERSON & Cpl. TOM COCHRAN

PHOTO ROBERT ASEN

THE GLENN MILLER BAND
playing for the troops in
England, prior to D Day.

GLENN MILLER
reported missing after flight,
December 1944.

When the legendary Ambrose decided to re-form his band as 'the largest and most expensive band yet for any nightclub', to play at London's 'Nightingale' club, Kenny found himself in the company of other young bloods including Johnny Dankworth, and Ronnie Scott, with arrangements by pianist Phil Cardew and Wally Stott. The irrepressible Kenny remembers the band well. 'We had a lot of fun in this job and Ammie found it was difficult to control such a bunch. So after a bit Bert offered me an extra fiver to look after the band when he wasn't there. After that he'd turn up for the

AMBROSE,
the name synonymous with the best food, the best service, the best music … and let's not talk about the price!

The Great Bandleaders

A King And A Prince Joined Ambrose's Band

"THE EMBASSY NEEDS YOU STOP COME BACK STOP EDWARD P."

That was the text of a cable that bandleader Bert Ambrose received while playing at the Clover Club in New York.

The sender was the Duke of Windsor.

Ambrose obeyed the command and returned to the famous Embassy Club in London to lead the band. So the Duke accomplished with one cable what the Embassy's owner had tried to do for months.

Ambrose, the man who gambled £25,000 on the turn of a single card, and who has earned an estimated million pounds during his life, started learning the violin at five. He went to America in 1914 and led bands in New York restaurants before returning to Britain in 1922 to lead at the Embassy Club.

In 1927 he went to the Mayfair Hotel, and returned to the Embassy in 1934. He became a household radio name and played at various London clubs and in variety until the war when he disbanded.

He re-formed at Ciro's Club in 1945 and is currently leading a dance band on tour.

Stars who were at one time with Ambrose include Vera Lynn, Anne Shelton, Sam Browne, Stanley Black, Johnny Dankworth, Kenny Baker, Ronnie Scott, Sid and Woolf Phillips, Ted Heath and Lew Stone.

Known as the friend of kings, queens and princes he has, as one writer put it, " something for which personality is a weak word."

AMBROSE.

Once at the Embassy the late King Alfonso of Spain and the Duke of Windsor asked to sit in with him on drums and bass. So Ambrose played violin and his pianist completed the quartet. An elderly dowager approached Ambrose and said, " What a delightful band, Mr Ambrose."

" Perhaps so," he replied, " but I'm afraid it would prove a little expensive."

DUNDEE EVENING TELEGRAPH, NOVEMBER 6TH 1951

first part of the evening, then disappear. He'd go home, saying he couldn't stand it. Eventually he gave up.' Kenny was upset when attending his funeral, to find that only six people were present. 'How sad, for a man who had been worshipped and respected in his day to pass almost un-noticed'.

Soon after leaving the Forces an opportunity arose to play with a band, the nucleus of which was to become the basis of Britain's most famous dance band. BBC Producer Pat Dixon had introduced a programme called *Top Ten* in which he invited various groups to perform, including Kenny's own band. Another such group was centred on the ex-Geraldo trombonist Ted Heath, who had decided to branch out with his own band, modelled on the big American swing bands. Kenny was soon to be lead trumpet and arranger for what was to become one of the finest swing bands of its era, the Ted Heath Orchestra.

Kenny enjoys a joke with Ambrose. A quiet man, Ambrose got what he wanted by such remarks as 'the saxes sound like a wart'.

PHOTO MELODY MAKER JUNE 9TH 1951

CHAPTER 4

THE TED HEATH BIG BAND YEARS
Bakerloo Non-Stop

T HE TED HEATH BAND had originated as a result of the young Ted being around for the war time visits of the Glenn Miller band and the Sam Donohue US Navy band. Both were superb examples of the disciplined , well arranged and driving bands typical of the American scene, and Ted felt that there was no British band to match them. This was something he intended to change, and as the war came to an end, he began carefully to recruit some of the best musicians around. Some were still in the armed forces, and Ted himself was playing with the Geraldo Orchestra. Ted Heath and his Music was a band that appeared as and when he could find the musicians, but nevertheless he was signed up for the BBC for a series entitled *Palestinian Half Hour*.

Obviously he had his eye on Kenny Baker who was known through his appearances with Ambrose, Maurice Winnick and others, and soon Kenny was signed up as lead trumpet with the newly formed Ted Heath Band. Many bandleaders signed the top musicians only for special recordings and

THE EARLY TED HEATH ORCHESTRA – 'you will appear on time, and will be smartly dressed'. Kenny in back row, third from left.

**THE ORIGINAL HEATH
BRASS SECTION.**
(LtoR) back row :
Alan Franks,
Harry Latham,
Kenny Baker,
Stan Roderick.
(LtoR) front row :
Jimmy Coombes,
Joe Cordell,
Harry Roche,
Jack Bentley.

broadcasts, but Ted was determined that his high standards would be maintained at all times. Expensive as it was, he placed them under contract, and thus ensured that the band was to obtain and keep the reputation he desired. For a time this meant that his bookings could often be at a loss, but he felt, and was proved right, that the long term benefits would justify his policy. With musicians of the calibre of Kenny and Jack Parnell, the band soon became known for the quality of it's music, and the Ted Heath Club was formed which rapidly obtained over five thousand members, an amazing figure for the day.

Not long before this, Ted had been busking in the streets of London, as he endeavoured to help with family support when work was difficult between the wars. Those days were now gone, and the immaculate, rather shy bandleader, was the image he was to have for the rest of his professional life.

All that Kenny had done in the past now came to be invaluable for this new venture. His reading of 'the dots' was perfect, his technique on the trumpet unsurpassed, and perhaps of most satisfaction to him was the opportunity to arrange for such a band. From now on *Sunday Night at the London Palladium* was awaited eagerly as this bright new band showed its paces. When Ted Heath asked Kenny for a show stopper, Kenny obliged with 'Bakerloo Non-Stop', a fast number which gave the band, and in particular the lead trumpet, the chance to show that here was a band to match any world-wide. A later concert at America's Carnegie Hall was to produce acclamation from the American public and press alike.

Decca were now producing fast selling records of the band, and the public loved 'Opus 1' and 'My Guy's Come Back'. BBC producer Pat Dixon, who later went on to produce the *Goon Show* and the highly successful *Baker's Dozen*, engaged the Heath Band for the popular 'Top Ten' series, and now nothing could stop them. Kenny speaks almost lovingly of their appearances at that famous of London dance halls, the Hammersmith Palais de Dance. Thousands of fans would jam this huge ballroom, and Monday nights were inevitably a sell out. Provincial venues such as Sherry's in Brighton told the same story, as attendance records were continually broken. Transport to venues was often uncertain. Kenny had an ancient Ford 8 which could not compare with Jack Parnell's sleek American limousine. However due to temperamental valves, the latter was often passed by Kenny, when the 'limo' was broken down yet again.

Christmas greetings 1947 to members of the Ted Heath Club. Some familiar names here, from jazz musicians to Lena Horne and a very young Petula Clark.

TED'S CHRISTMAS CARD

TED'S CHRISTMAS CARD 1949
Musician and humorous artist Gerard Hoffnung designed this Christmas card for Ted and Moira
Heath in 1949. Could Kenny be the trumpet player in the snow covered tower?

A popular feature of the Ted Heath shows was the 'band within a band' which put the spotlight on the Kenny Baker Swing Group. The personnel varied from time to time, but might consist of Kenny on trumpet, Harry Roche (trombone), Reg Owen (clarinet), Norman Stenfalt (piano), Charlie Short (bass), and of course Jack Parnell on drums. What a collection of talent.

Oddly enough, both Kenny and his new friend Jack Parnell felt that Ted was more in favour of music strictly for dancing, and often they would call out for more jazz. They felt that they would prefer the hard swinging sound of the wartime Sam Donahue band, to the disciplined precision of the Glenn Miller sound. In Ted's defence, he liked the jazz, but knew that the public was not ready for too much. A happy compromise was worked out, and no-one complained. The band was not too impressed when appearing on one of the early ATV productions from Alexandra Palace. Shiny instruments had to be dulled, the musicians were made up with grey pastel make-up, and after much waiting about, they decided that TV (then in black and white) was not as glamorous as they had been told.

BBC TELEVISION BALL
at the Hammersmith Palais
– the Ted Heath big band
in action.

No prizes for guessing who. The nineteen year old Dickie Valentine during his 'try-out' period with the Heath band.

Big bands equals one night stands. Kenny spends part of the journey working on a new band arrangement in a quiet corner of the dining car.

JACK PARNELL –
a great character, as well as a fine drummer.

Although Kenny was happy with the working conditions and pay of the Heath Band, he began to tire of the repeated programmes that were a feature of big bands, and after three years he approached Ted with a view to leaving the band. Ted found it hard to accept that his lead trumpet and arranger could want to leave, but Kenny was adamant. Ted asked if it was finance, and Kenny replied that money was not an aspect he had considered. He was just conscious that with much repetition of everything in the band library, he was becoming stale. He knew every arrangement by heart, and even his solos were beginning to lose their sparkle. In 1948 he left what has been described as one of the best swing bands of its time, to freelance, and in particular to form a small group without the hassles of the large organisation associated with a band the size of the Heath Orchestra. An approach was made to Maynard Ferguson, then playing with Stan Kenton, to take Kenny's place, but this was turned down.

THE KENNY BAKER SWING GROUP –
the 'band within a band'
of the Heath Orchestra.
Charlie Short (bass),
Jack Parnell (drums),
Norman Stenfalt (piano),
Kenny (trumpet),
Harry Roche (trombone),
Reg Owen (clarinet),
Johnny Gray (sax).

8th DECEMBER ———— 1947 ———— 20th DECEMBER

Introducing

♫ **TED HEATH and his MUSIC** ♫

featuring

PAUL CARPENTER - *Vocalist and Compere*

JACK PARNELL

KENNY BAKER

DAVE WILKINS

at the

BARBECUE

WESTOVER ROAD, BOURNEMOUTH

Telephone - Bournemouth 6414

SOUVENIR PROGRAMME

A sign of the times is highlighted not so much by the 1947 programme, but by the 'a la carte menu' available at the venue in Bournemouth. Wartime rationing was still in operation, so did you really only get one sardine ?!

REFRESHMENTS

A LA CARTE

SOUPS
PEA TOMATO OX TAIL	......	6d.

SNACKS
CORNISH PASTIE, PEAS, POTATOES		I/6
HAMBURG, CARROTS, POTATOES		I/9
BEANS ON TOAST WITH POTATOES		I/-
SPAGHETTI ON TOAST WITH POTATOES		I/-
SARDINE ON TOAST WITH POTATOES	......	I/-
WELSH RAREBIT WITH POTATOES		I/3
CANAPES VARIOUS (COLD)	....	8d.

SWEETS
VANILLA TRIFLE	......	9d.
FRUIT JELLY AND CREAM	......	6d.
BAKED DATE SLICE	....	6d.
CREAM GATEAU	....	6d.
VANILLA ICES		6d.
STRAWBERRY ICES	......	6d.
MIXED ICES	......	I/-

Ted Heath venues –

Hippodrome, Birmingham
City Hall, Sheffield
Brangwyn Hall, Swansea
Gaumont State, Kilburn
Glasgow Empire
Kingston Empire
Blackpool Empire
London Palladium (many times)
Wood Green Empire
Liverpool Empire
Guildhall, Southampton
Nottingham Empire
Golders Green Hippodrome
South Parade Pier, Portsmouth
Croydon Empire
Embassy Cinema, Clifton
Central Hall, Bristol
Central Pier, Blackpool
Stoll Theatre
Drill Hall, Northampton
Lonsdale Cinema, Carlisle
Hippodrome, Coventry
Barbecue, Bournemouth
Villa Marina, Isle of Man
The Adelphi, London
and many others …

The immaculate Ted Heath - a good disciplinarian, but popular with it.

PHOTO CHRIS HAYES

THE KENNY BAKER BAND, 1951.
From the left,
Vic Ash,
Jimmy Skidmore,
Tubby Hayes (aged 16),
Kenny,
Pete Bray(drums),
singer Lynda Ellington &
Alan McDonald (bass).
The event was a special jazz
show for schoolchildren.

The new group started in 1949 was the Kenny Baker Band, and had Kenny as leader and on trumpet, Jimmy Skidmore, Vic Ash and Harry Klein on saxes, Dave Milne on piano, Alan McDonald on bass and Pete Bray on drums. He later added another sax player, the sixteen year old Tubby Hayes.

1951 saw the Sextet 'on the road' and with it came one of the perils of one night stands. The coach in which the band was travelling left the road near Nuneaton and smashed into a tree, and as a result Kenny sustained a fractured third finger on his right hand. Not a major problem for the average person, but in the case of a trumpet player it could have been disastrous. Kenny announced that the tour would continue, 'under limited circumstances', and in typical Baker fashion promptly taught himself to play with the two undamaged fingers on his right hand ,together with the first finger of the left hand. Other members of the group hurt in the smash were altoist Vic Ash (lacerated nose), tenor man Jimmy Skidmore (bruised and lacerated arm) and bass player Alan McDonald (bruised ankle). Singer Joan Brook had a suspected skull fracture but no injury was found. Tubby Hayes was not hurt. The show went on.

Baker and four of Sextet injured in coach smash

Snapped almost immediately after they had climbed down from the shattered coach are four of the Baker Sextet: l. to r., Pete Bray, Dave Milne, Jimmy Skidmore and Tubby Hayes.

The coach crash which could have stopped a few careers. From the left, Pete Bray, Dave Milne, Jimmy Skidmore, and Tubby Hayes. Several of the sextet had some injury, from scratches to fractures.

TRUMPET-LEADER Kenny Baker sustained a fractured finger in a serious road smash three miles from Nuneaton, Warwickshire, early on Sunday (19th).

He and his Sextet were returning from a dance at Fenton. Stoke-on-Trent, when their coach crashed head-on into a tree.

Shielding his face with his hands, Kenny was flung heavily forward and the third finger of his right hand was fractured.

Doctors at Middlesex Hospital have managed to place the injured finger in plaster without restricting the use of the others,

(Continued on page 6)

Kenny Baker leaves the Middlesex Hospital after treatment for his fracture.

Leonard Munsie seriously hurt

Yet another road smash involved Leonard Munsie, Exploitation Manager of Messrs. Bosworth's and also well-known as a saxist. He was seriously hurt when returning last Sunday from an engagement with Bunny May's Orchestra.

Leonard's car was overturned in the accident, and he sustained multiple injuries. He is at present in St. Mary Abbotts Hospital, Kensington, London, W.8.

of the songs she sings.

On September 1 the Gill band plays a one-night-stand at the Eagle Flying Club, Tollerton.

BAKER

(Continued from page 1)
and Kenny announces that he will continue his engagements "under limited circumstances."

The Sextet commenced a ten-day tour on Wednesday (22nd), which will take them to Nelson (Friday), Bedworth (Saturday), Dudley (Sunday) and a week in Scotland, starting at Dingwall on Monday. Kenny will play trumpet as much as his injury will permit.

Other members of his band hurt in the smash were altoist Vic Ash (lacerated nose), bassist Alan McDonald (bruised ankle) and tenorist Jimmy Skidmore (bruised and lacerated arm).

Vocalist Joan Brook suffered a severe blow on the head and was X-rayed for suspected fracture of the skull. Fortunately, no injury was discovered, but Joan felt delayed after-effects of the smash on Sunday night, when the band appeared at the Feldman Club.

She suffered a minor nervous breakdown, but after a few days rest she has now recovered.

Kenny with fractured middle finger resulting from the coach crash. It didn't stop him, he taught himself a new fingering technique, two fingers on normal hand, and one finger on the other!

MELODY MAKER AUGUST 25TH 1951

1   Opus One
2   The Very Thought Of You
3   Cossack Patrol
4   My Guy's Come Back
5   Twilight Time
6   First Jump
7   East Of the Sun
8   Not So Quiet Please
9   Wotcher! (Knocked 'Em
     In the Old Kent Road)
10 Backerloo Non-Stop
11 Skyliner
12 Opus One
13 Moto Perpetua
14 Pompton Turnpike
15 Song Of The Volga
     Boatman
16 Eager Beaver
17 On The Atcheson,
     Topeka & Santa Fe
18 11.60 P.M.
19 Ring Dem Bells
20 Lullaby Of Broadway
21 Going Nowhere
22 Any Old Iron
23 On Ilkla Moor Baht'At
24 Donegal Cradle Song
25 My Heart Goes Crazy

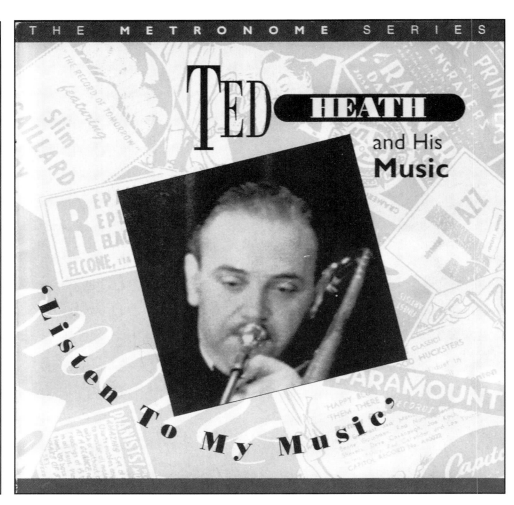

The Metronome Series, HEP Records CD 52, Mono 1997.

"Ted Heath's boys play with tremendous attack and enthusiasm and their brass section was one of the best I've ever heard, and I'm not forgetting Miller or Donahue … Ted is well on his way to opening a new era in British swing music."

Roy Sonin, Editor,
Melody Maker, October, 1945.

All went well as the band toured the country until Kenny had to take doctor's advice to give up playing temporarily in order to sort out a hernia that had developed. The band was disbanded and an advert shortly appeared in the musical press :

Bedford van 28 ex WD 15cwt brake, which seats nine or ten people, plus room for bass, drums etc. Any enterprising bandleader contact Kenny Baker, Middlesex Hospital.

After successful surgery and during convalescence, Kenny was approached by Lew Stone to play in his band in the Pigalle Restaurant in Piccadilly, and he accepted. Kenny was later delighted to receive an invitation from the BBC to form a new band to take part in an experimental show to be produced by Pat Dixon, the band to be called 'The Baker's Dozen', and the show to be called *Let's Settle for Music*. He jumped at the chance.

CHAPTER 5

LET'S SETTLE FOR MUSIC
With The Kenny Baker's Dozen

BAKER TO LEAD STAR 'DOZEN' IN NO-POP AIR SERIES

MELODY MAKER APRIL 19TH 1952.

THIS HEADLINE was an early warning that the BBC was about to provide a little more jazz for the starving listeners, and the article went on to quote Kenny : 'This is a fulfilment of an ambition I have had for years, – a programme of interesting music, no pops, and none of the dreary "boom-ching" noises heard so often on the air today.'

The new show was to be called *Let's Settle for Music* and was the original brain-child of BBC producer Pat Dixon. He was the man who had introduced the nation to *The Goons*, and *Breakfast/Bedtime with Braden*. Although not a musician, he knew what he wanted, and recognised that Kenny Baker was the man to lead a band made up of the best British musicians of the day. The music was to be live, and was to appeal to the many

'THE KENNY BAKER'S DOZEN',
(LtoR)
**Tommy McQuater,
Keith Christie,
George Chisholm,
Harry Gold
(dep for Poggy Pogson)
Harry Klein, Derek Collins,
Keith Bird, Harry Hayes,
Kenny Baker, Derek Smith,
Bill Le Sage, Phil Seamen,
Alan Mack dep
for Joe Muddel.**

One of Britain's great entertainers. George Chisholm brought his humorous talents as well as superb trombone playing to the Dozen.

jazz fans who were suffering from too much 'boom-ching', and a plethora of singing stars who made money, but whose commercialism often got in the way of the musical content for which Pat knew there was a demand. The early line-ups varied as previous commitments affected personnel, and as Kenny's arrangements called for various groupings. But we were likely to find what was to be called 'The Kenny Baker's Dozen', to be made up from such as Freddie Ballerini, Keith Bird, Harry Hayes, Harry Klein, and the redoubtable E.O. Pogson, (reeds); Poggy also played on a variety of strange instruments often of his own design, and Freddie Ballerini also featured on violin; Harry Roche was on trombone, later to be replaced by George Chisholm; Tommy McQuater, and Freddie Clayton, backed up the maestro Kenny Baker on trumpets; Frank Clark on bass; Pat Dodd on piano, replaced by Bill McGuffie at a later date; Martin Slavin on vibes; Eric Delaney, drums. All the personnel were picked by Pat Dixon with Kenny's approval. There were to be no singers – the make up of the band represented all the 'stars' that were needed. Certainly listeners could not have wished for a more illustrious collection of British jazz musicians.

The first broadcast was on April 19th 1952, and was well received, although Kenny had the frustration of not being able to play due to his recent hernia operation. Tommy McQuater took the trumpet lead, while Kenny conducted the band through his own arrangements of mainly 'oldies'. The announcer was Wilfrid Thomas, an Australian whose gentle commentary fitted in well with the general nature of the show, with little in the way of some of the more puerile ramblings we have had to become used to.

An unusually pensive Kenny Baker, shot during one of the legendary 'Let's Settle For Music' broadcasts from the BBC Paris Studios in Regent Street.

Kenny's original brief had been rather vague, – 'Get down to the studio, write down a few routines and we'll put you on live.' This procedure proved nightmarish for Kenny, who had to direct a group playing improvised music live, but which had to finish to the precise time dictated by Pat Dixon, always at the end of the signature tune – Pat did not like 'fade-outs'. 'You can't expect ad lib jazz and perfect timing' protested Kenny. After two weeks it was agreed by producer and musicians that the formula was nerve wracking and not working. So a tighter programme with timed arrangements was used, which still gave the musicians the chance to play improvised jazz, but guaranteed a predictable ending time for the programme. Once Kenny and Pat had agreed the make-up of the show, Kenny made the arrangements, and passed them on to his copyist Syd Cordell . With the skills of arranger, copyist and musicians, rehearsal times could be a minimum, and a sound check and quick run through led straight to the live performance.

By now the Dozen was proving very popular, and Tuesday night at 10.20pm on the Light Programme, was eagerly awaited by fans who welcomed this addition to a fairly meagre ration of jazz on the BBC. Poggy Pogson, when not toying with one of his non standard wind instruments, described the sessions as 'madly amusing, it takes you back twenty years to

Producer Pat Dixon in the Control Room at Broadcasting House. A keen jazz fan , he persuaded the powers that be at the BBC that 'Let's Settle for Music' would be a winner. How right he was.

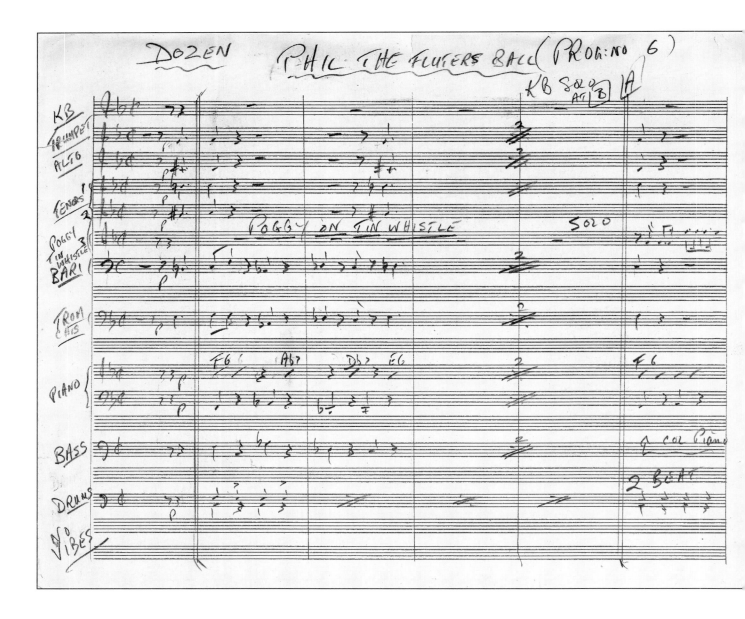

The Baker arrangements were used for most of the band's output, and the hand written master copy was handed over to Syd Cordell for rewriting for each musician.

the wonderful days before everything got spoiled with commercialisation and vocals. I'd play this date for nothing.'

What had been started as a programme experiment was soon to be extended again and again. A year after *Melody Maker*'s opening fanfare, the same paper was adding another headline, this time describing *Let's Settle for Music* as :

RADIO'S NUMBER ONE JAZZ SHOW

Describing the producer Pat Dixon as 'someone who looked every bit the boffin who delved in nuclear physics', the article goes on to describe Pat's approach as a wish to produce a programme 'that makes good listening for those really interested in good dance music, something better than the average tripe they put out … generally our numbers are not on the plug list, and

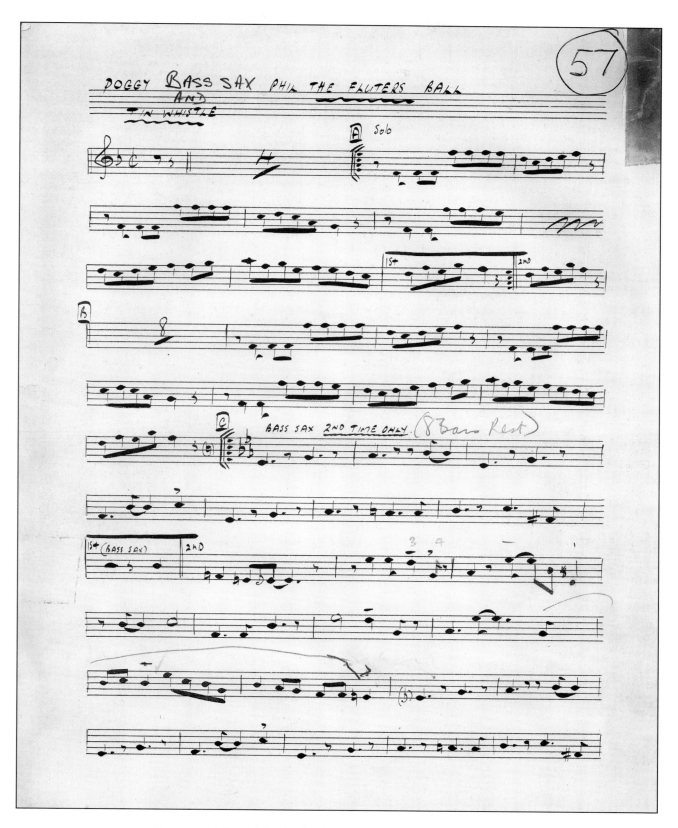

Bass sax and tin whistle line for Poggy Pogson in 'Phil the Fluter's Ball'.

February 14, 1953   MELODY MAKER   5

MIKE NEVARD dissects—
RADIO'S NUMBER ONE JAZZ SHOW

THE man in the doorway was tall, wiry and gangling. He had grey fluffy hair, a dome of a forehead. He looked every bit the boffin who delved in nuclear physics.

He didn't look like the man responsible for Britain's brightest jazz broadcasts. But he is.

He is Pat Dixon, originator and producer of the Tuesday night series. Let's Settle For Music.

The start

The tweed-clad giant hulloed gruffly, spun on a heel, and disappeared into the room. It was then we saw Kenny Baker. We should have noticed him before. It was his flat.

"Come in," said Kenny, holding back the door. We passed the scent of rich cooking and entered the tiny lounge.

This was where the programme started. Every Friday, Pat brought along his list of suggestions; Kenny trotted out a few of his own.

From the mêlée, 13 numbers would evolve. And Kenny would write 13 arrangements.

"Yes, everything's written," said Kenny. "Sometimes we play numbers we've used before. There's a whole pile of them there." He pointed to a sagging shelf.

We asked Pat the policy behind his series.

The policy

"We're not out to prove anything," he said. "Our aim is to produce a programme that makes good listening for those really interested in good dance music. Something better than the average tripe they put out.

"We only use the tunes we consider good tunes—and we go back a long way to get them.

But that doesn't mean we don't use new numbers. We had one last week—'Quiet Man.'

"But generally they're numbers not on the plug list. And the pluggers can't understand it."

Kenny took up the theme. "You see, we get the right men to interpret them," he said. "Every musician is on the programme because he is experienced, and because he knows what we want."

We saw what he meant four

The men who make Let's Settle For Music. Producer Pat Dixon and leader-arranger Kenny Baker.

days later when the boys started rehearsal. There were twelve musicians, six microphones. That's how they get that bright, clean sound. Drummer Eric Delaney was the only man without amplification—and he used it the other week.

On this session there was a mike for pianist Bill McGuffie, one for bassist Frank Clarke, one for vibes player Martin Slavin, one for Kenny, one between brassmen Harry Roche and Tommy McQuater, and one for the assorted sax section—Poggy Pogson, Freddy Ballerini, Keith Bird, Harry Hayes and Harry Klein.

The production

Could you get a more assorted team? Yet the result . . . well, you only have to watch a rehearsal to see just why this is the most relaxed jazz series since Jazz Is Where You Find It.

"Not fast enough" calls Dixon from the control box as they take one number. "No, get that lazy sound" as they take another.

Harry Klein jumps up for a solo and the band bay satirically like a pack of wolves.

Some of the numbers they run through only once. And you saw what Dixon meant when he said "We try to keep the interest going through every number. We don't give the listener time to adjust his shoe-laces."

In between numbers, they joke and laugh. As Martin Slavin said afterwards:

"It's like a big happy family. Everyone puts everything he's got into the session."

Martin earns his bread and butter MD-ing at Selby's. "But it's great to go back and dig out bits of Rollini and Goodman and Venuti," he says.

The opinions

Poggy Pogson, grand-old-timer of the saxmen, described the sessions as:

"Madly amusing. It takes you back 20 years to the wonderful days before commercialism and vocals.

"I'd play this date for nothing."

And that's how they all feel. No one regards Let's Settle For Music as a job. It's a return to the Good Old Days when jazz was jazz and Pat Dixon was a young man.

And that's why the Tuesday night series is building up a new legion of fans for British dance bands, as well as reassuring those with flagging faith that Britain *can* produce good jazz.

And the secret is that nobody's sticking to the rules of Dixieland, bop or any of the other cults. They are all out to play good, listenable jazz.

And did I mention that late-forties radio show Jazz Is Where You Find It? Check back and see who produced it. Pat Dixon.

The two best jazz shows in a decade isn't bad going for a man who looks as if he's going to lead in "Strut Miss Lizzie" with one hand while he splits the atom with the other.

At the top—Eric Delaney and Frank Clarke. Under the "Show"—tenorman Keith Bird and altoist Harry Hayes.

Contrasts in the saxes—tenorman Freddy Ballerini and alto-baritone-sarist Harry Klein.

The veteran stalwart of the sax team—Poggy Pogson. Playing up there at the back are trombonist Harry Roche and trumpeter Tommy McQuater. Altogether, a quarter of Baker's Dozen.

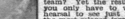

Vibes player Martin Slavin at a Let's Settle For Music rehearsal. "It's like a big, happy family," he says.

The pencil smoker — Bill McGuffie. The Show Band pianist has his own solo spot in the Baker series.

'RADIO'S NUMBER ONE JAZZ SHOW'.
Melody Maker
February 14th, 1953.

Announcer Wilfrid Thomas (right) checks over the *Let's Settle for Music* running order with Kenny.

Mike Nevard dissects –

RADIO'S NUMBER ONE JAZZ SHOW

THE MAN in the doorway was tall, wiry and gangling. He had grey fluffy hair, a dome of a forehead. He looked every bit the boffin who delved in nuclear physics.

He didn't look like the man responsible for Britain's brightest jazz broadcasts. But he is.

He is Pat Dixon, originator and producer of the Tuesday night series *Let's Settle For Music.*

The start

The tweed-clad giant hulloed gruffly, spun on a heel, and disappeared into the room. It was then we saw Kenny Baker. We should have noticed him before. It was his flat.

"Come in." said Kenny, holding back the door. We passed the scent of rich cooking and entered the tiny lounge.

This was where the programme started. Every Friday, Pat brought along his list of suggestions; Kenny trotted out a few of his own.

From the mélée, 13 numbers would evolve. And Kenny would write 13 arrangements.

"Yes, everything's written," said Kenny. "Sometimes we play numbers we've used before. There's a whole pile of them there." He pointed to a sagging shelf.

We asked Pat the policy behind his series.

The policy

"We're not out to prove anything," he said. "Our aim is to produce a programme that makes good listening for those really interested in good dance music. something better than the average tripe they put out.

"We only use the tunes we consider good tunes—and we go back a long way to get them. But that doesn't mean we don't use new numbers. We had one last week— 'Quiet Man.'

"But generally they're numbers

not on the plug list. And the pluggers can't understand it."

Kenny took up the theme, "You see, we get the right men to interpret them," he said. Every musician

EXTRA NINE WEEKS FOR BAKER'S DOZEN

POPULARITY of the Kenny Baker "Baker's Dozen" radio programme is once again emphasised by the extension of its present series of airings for another nine weeks.

Due to end on March 11. after a series of seven broadcasts, it will now last until May 13, and longer if a second option is taken up by the BBC.

Kenny is to record some special sides for Phillips, accompanied by full orchestra directed by Wally Stott. These will present him in an entirely new musical setting.

Kenny Baker recently dubbed the sound track for a Douglas Fairbanks TV film which will be shown only in the United States.

is on the programme because he is experienced, and because he knows what we want."

We saw what he meant four days later when the boys started rehearsal. There were twelve musicians, six microphones. That's how they get that bright, clean sound. Drummer Eric Delaney was the only man without amplification—and he used it the other week.

On this session there was a mike for pianist Bill McGuffie, one for bassist Frank Clarke, one for vibes player Martin Slavin, one for Kenny, one between brassmen Harry Roche and Tommy McQater, and one for the assorted sax section— Poggy Pogson, Freddy Ballerini, Keith Bird, Harry Hayes and Harry Klein.

The production

Could you get a more assorted team? Yet the result ... well, you only have to watch a rehearsal to see just why this is the most relaxed jazz series since *Jazz Is Where You Find It.*

"Not fast enough" calls Dixon from the control box as they take one number. "No, get that lazy sound" as they take another.

Harry Klein jumps up for a solo and the band bay satirically like a pack of wolves.

Some of the numbers they run through only once. and you saw what Dixon meant when he said "We try to keep the interest going through every number. We don't give the listener time to adjust his shoe-laces."

In between numbers, they joke and laugh. As Martin Slavin said afterwards:

"It's like a big happy family. Everyone puts everything he's got into the session."

Martin earns his bread and butter MD-ing at Selby's. "But it's great to go back and dig out bits of Rollini and Goodman and Venuti," he says.

The opinions

Poggy Pogson, grand-old-timer of the saxmen, described the sessions as:

"Madly amusing. It takes you back 20 years to the wonderful days before everything got spoiled with commercialism and vocals. I'd play this date for nothing."

And that's how they all feel. No one regards *Let's Settle For Music* as a job. It's a return to the Good Old Days when jazz was jazz and Pat Dixon was a young man.

And that's why the Tuesday night series is building up a new legion of fans for the British dance bands, as well as reassuring those with flagging faith that Britain can produce good jazz.

And the secret is that nobody's sticking to the rules of Dixieland, bop or any of the other cults. They are all out to play good listenable jazz

And did I mention that late-forties radio show Jazz Is Where You Find It? Check back and see who produced it, Pat Dixon.

The two best jazz shows in a decade isn't bad going for a man who looks as if he's going to lead in "Strut Miss Lizzie" with one hand while he splits the atom with the other.

Peter Sellers and Spike Milligan, "Finalists in the Brass Band Contest (Economy Section) – Scunthorpe Municipal Baths." Keen supporters of the studio based Dozen, they would drop in between rehearsals.

PHOTO SPIKE MILLIGAN COLLECTION

the pluggers can't understand it'. It's interesting to note that the output was described as 'good dance music'. No doubt it was, but listening to it in 1998, just makes us realise that here was a lovely jazz sound, not trad, not bebop, but using the best of those contesting branches of jazz. Among other reissues is a CD by Lake Records of recordings by the 'Half Dozen', and 'Jazz Today' group, and it is a joy to hear George Chisholm, Dill Jones and Bruce Turner in their heyday.

Pat's instruction to 'play what you like as long as it's good' kept the musicians and the public happy. Kenny is positive that the ideas stemmed from Pat Dixon, and the jazz men simply delivered what Pat felt sounded right. The control of what was going on and the sound of the band, was taken by the producer in the control room listening closely, and deciding what was good and what wasn't. Although the broadcasts were all from a studio with no audience, there was one person who dropped in whenever he could, and that was Spike Milligan, himself a keen trumpet player - occasionally he was joined by erstwhile drummer Peter Sellers.

One of the strengths of Baker's Dozen was in the gradual change of style as Pat felt appropriate - the idea of using the Eric Delaney battery of timps was his, but Kenny was the man with the skills to incorporate this sound into his arrangements. The music style of the Dozen was never static, as the ensemble was changed to reflect the big band brass sound of the Ellington and Basie bands. By the mid fifties the band make-up included three trumpets, two trombones, five saxes, vibes and rhythm section - rather more than a dozen, but no one was counting. Life was also made easier as the Musicians' Union relaxed its views on recordings, and the programme could be recorded one day and broadcast the next. For Kenny, flying by the seat of his trousers during a live radio show became more a thing of the past.

An indication of the popularity of the show was clear from the shouts of protest that occurred each time there was a threat to replace it with something more like the quieter offerings of *Housewives' Choice*. These threats resulted in further headlines,

WHY BANISH THE KENNY BAKER SHOW FROM THE AIR?

MELODY MAKER MARCH 28TH 1953.

Claims were made that the BBC made no attempt to monitor listeners' reactions, and so were not aware that many potential listeners were turning to foreign stations which were more generous in their output of 'dance music', rather than the light pop music which tended to predominate the BBC produced air waves. If you were so minded you could listen to the ten best selling songs in 1954, which were :

These were hardly appealing to the more up-tempo members of the public, who found in *Let's Settle for Music* something more demanding and satisfying, and to whom the loss of that programme would have ruined the week. Things looked encouraging again when the paper reported :

**BBC TO RESUME BAKERS DOZEN
AND GERALDO'S TIP TOP TUNES.
...RECOMMENCING ON JANUARY 28TH, 1954.**

Joy was short lived as the rumblings continued, this time the headline of protest in the *Melody Maker* edition of February 6th 1954 stating :

HEADS IN THE SAND AT THE BBC!

Music critic and jazz musician Maurice Burman described the Kenny Baker's Dozen as "a band far removed from today's hit tunes, publicity agents, band bookers, managers, and Big Business; a band for the sake of it, and jazz for the love of it". The style had caught on and as Burman wrote in the March

1953 *Melody Maker*, "I can't remember a time this side of the forties when a band pleased so utterly every section of the listening public". Quite a statement, but there was no doubt that most at that time would agree with his comments. He continues : " … for once we had a band that played no plugs, but only the best and most suitable tunes, that did not care about trads, mods and sectarian bods, that had a good compère to read a good script, that had great soloists who had created a tremendous interest, and that plays dance-music-cum jazz in a free and thoroughly satisfactory way. And how does the BBC react? By taking it off … I believe I am voicing the opinion of millions when I say – **BAKER MUST RETURN**."

Baker did return, and kept on returning, so that what had been planned as six broadcasts continued for seven years. A last quote from Burman sums up his views at the time: "Kenny is amazing. He plays any style with conviction and ease. There is no other player in Europe who can do it."

At the same time Douglas Enefer, journalist with the *Evening Chronicle*, was writing :

> *Mr. Kenny Baker - the greatest trumpet man in the country and among the top brass anywhere - is writing new arrangements for his famous 'Baker's Dozen' … for long regarded as the best band series on the air. It is becoming tiresomely repetitive to say that Mr. Baker is among the greatest trumpeters on either side of the Atlantic - but if there is any other way to describe this remarkable virtuoso, I do not know what it may be.*

Meanwhile Jack Baverstock of the *New Musical Express* was writing:

> *To Kenny Baker and his Dozen must go credit and the blessing of all who are discerning in their dance music, for every Tuesday evening it is possible to hear a handpicked group of top fully experienced professional musicians, led by an acknowledged Master-Instrumentalist, playing custom-built arrangements of tunes, old, new, hits, misses, in a manner that restores one's faith in this music business of ours. And the result? … some first class modern jazz, modern yet devoid of the eternal bop touches, with a kick more usually associated with two beat bands.*

It is interesting at this distance of time to note the references to the raging trad versus bop war, from which Kenny held himself aloof, contenting himself with using the best of these jazz styles, with no excesses. It is also odd to see references to the 'dance music' played by the Dozen, surely something that described the strict tempo of the Victor Sylvester band, but not the swinging Baker ensemble which was never intended to play in a dance hall, or even in front of a live audience. With its scheduled radio time on a Tuesday evening, it was music to listen to, even if occasionally we rolled up

> ## *"Kenny is amazing. He plays any style with conviction and ease. There is no other player in Europe who can do it."*
>
> MUSIC CRITIC AND JAZZ MUSICIAN MAURICE BURMAN

DOZEN. 6th SERIES. STARTING. JAN 1st 57 | Syd Cordell £23-6-0 Jan 57 / 14 13 0 March 3 57 / 21 1 6 April 1st 57

NAME	FEE £135-0-0 JAN 1st 57 FEE PAYED	£135 JAN 8th 57	£135 JAN 15	£135 JAN 22	£135 Jan 29	£135 Feb 5th	£135 Feb 12th
T. Mcquater	7 - -	T Mc 7	T Mc 7	TM 7	TM 7	TM 7	TM 7
G. Chis	7 - -	Chis 7	Chis 7	Chis 7	Chis	Chis	Chis
K. Shiite	7 -	K Shiite 7	K Johns 7	K Wll 7	K Wll	Ken Wray	K Wray
H. Hayes	7 - -	H Hayes 7	H Hayes 7	H H 7	H H	H H	H H
K. Bird	7 - -	K Bird 7	K Bird 7	KB 7	KB	KB	KB
Derek Collins	7 - -	D Collins 7	D Collins 7	D Col 7	D Col	D Col	D Col
E.O. Pogson (p)	7 10	Harry Gold 7 10	Poggy 7 10	Pog 7 10	Pog 7 10	Pog 7 10 -	H Gold 7 10
H Klein	7 -	H Klein 7	H Klein 7	H K 7	H K 7	H K 7	H K 7
D. Smith	7 - -	DS 7	D Smith 7	DS 7	DS 7	DS 7	DS 7
Alan Mack (p)	7 10	G. Mack 7 10	Al Mack 7 10	Lennie Bush 7 10 -	L Bush 7 10	L Bush 7 10 -	L Bush 7 10
Phil Seaman (p)	7 10	P S 7 10	P Seam 7 10	P. Seam 7 co	P S 9	P S 7	Tony Kinsey 7
B. Le Sage	7 10	B L Sage 7 10	B L Sage 7 10	B Le S 7 10	B Le S	B Le S -	B Le S
	£86	£86	£86	£86	£86	£86	£86-0-0

The Dozen's accounts in Kenny's handwriting, show the pay received by the band.

the carpet and jived to such as George Chisholm and colleagues.

An interesting sidelight on the finances of the Dozen was in the accounts which Kenny painstakingly kept. The table for the series starting in January 1957 shows that the BBC paid a total of £86 for twelve of Britain's top musicians, with most getting £7 for a programme. Those with a special facility such as being able to double up on instruments were paid £7.10.0. (an extra 50p in today's money!) The names are also a roll call of musicians who we have seen become increasingly important to the UK jazz scene. Some have sadly passed on, others are still giving enormous pleasure to audiences around the country.

Although in the early days the Dozen was rarely let out of the broadcasting studio, it was used, of all places, in the BBC's *Saturday Night Theatre* in *Celery Quarter Blues*, a play adapted from Frederic Raphael's novel about the rise to stardom of a greengrocer's son. The lead was taken by Jim Dale, better known as heart-throb, pop singer and star of 'Carry On' films, and the 'hot band' to accompany him was the Baker's Dozen. Music was specially commissioned for the occasion, but didn't make the Charts. The band was also used in the film *Trumpet Story*, referred to in chapter 7.

By 1957 the size of the band had increased to sixteen, although the name remained unchanged as 'The Dozen'. The size of band enabled Pat Dixon to provide music as played by the American bands, such as Count Basie and Duke Ellington, and once again Kenny was able to demonstrate his talent for arranging with the big band material now requested by the producer. One such line-up included Stan Reynolds, Albert Hall and Jo Hunter (trumpets); Bill Geldard and Eddie Harvey (trombones); Don Rendell, John Scott, Poggy Pogson, Harry Klein, and Harry Hayes (saxes); Jack Seymour (bass); Norman Stenfalt (piano); Tony Kinsey (drums); Bill Le Sage (vibes). With this sort of personnel, it was hardly surprising that the British public were able to feel that, Ted Heath aside, there were no other bands who could deliver the swinging, hard driving music associated with American records. The line-up changed continually over the seven years, as Pat Dixon suggested numerous different musicians such as Bill McGuffie, Ralph Dollimore, and Phil Seamen.

Things had been going so well when tragedy struck with the unexpected death of producer Pat Dixon at the age of 56 in October 1958. Kenny had always claimed that the quality of the show was due to the influence of Pat, who knew what he wanted, and accepted no compromise. He was of course fortunate in having Kenny Baker, who was able to make certain that he got arrangements and performances of the highest standard. There were worries, well founded, that the demise of Pat would mean the end of *Let's Settle for Music*. When he joined the BBC he had rebelled against the Corporation's attitude to jazz, and was strong-minded enough to make his masters accept that here was a music that was wanted by large numbers of the public, who were loud in their support of the music of The Dozen. The fact that he was the person behind the Ted Heath radio show, as well as *The Goons, Breakfast with Braden* and then *Let's Settle for Music*, showed that here was a man happy to strive for 'different' programmes, and who generally succeeded in getting past the bureaucracy of the BBC. As was said in one of the many tributes at the time, 'Jazz has lost a great ally; the BBC a great producer.' Perhaps a typically generous comment of Kenny says it all – 'no one replaced his special something which kept the band in the public eye and ear. He made it what it was. I made the music, but he created The Dozen.'

Melody Maker of December 1958 headlines now shouted :

WHY KILL THE BAKER'S DOZEN?

Is the Kenny Baker Dozen programme *Let's Settle for Music* to die at the end of its present run?
For the past eight years it has been regarded by the serious jazz student as one of the BBC's finest jazz productions. Said producer John Burnaby, who

took over from Pat Dixon, "I obviously cannot comment on BBC policy. I can only say that as far as I know it is coming off … I shall be constantly fighting to bring it back."

A few days later the *Melody Maker* headline ran :

REPRIEVE FOR BAKER'S DOZEN?

The Kenny Baker Dozen may be reprieved by BBC Governor Jim Davidson. Kenny has stated …'We will probably be back with a much smaller band, maybe eight or nine piece. Jim Davidson told me he wants to get away from the usual big band sound … The cost of the present series is too high for the audience it could command on its late night Tuesday airings … I pointed out that a better timing, such as that used by the Billy Cotton Band Show, would send our listening figures up enormously. For the time being the Tuesday slot is to be used by the Ted Heath Band.'

But it was not to be, and as had been predicted, *Let's Settle for Music* never appeared again. Jazz audiences were once again having to search the *Radio Times* for their music which was in such short supply.

As one disgruntled reader wrote to the *New Musical Express*,

> *Something worse than Rock and Roll has happened to British Dance music! What used to be the only high quality programme in a welter of Tin Pan Alley mediocrities - Kenny Baker's Dozen- was foully murdered the other evening. … In its place, no doubt, we shall have some reliable hack, with a well loved plug list, and the usual musical zombies beloved of the BBC.*

RALPH JEFFERY, LEEDS.

And from the *Exeter Express*, Noel Watford stated

> *Make no mistake about it, this programme is Radio Three material if room cannot be found on the Light Programme. In a way it is chamber music - specialised and of high quality, and absolutely indispensable to the discerning listener who gets little pleasure from skiffle, strict tempo or sighing singers.*

In spite of a lot of similar support, the *Let's Settle for Music* programme and the associated Baker's Dozen disappeared at the end of Pat Dixon's last series on December 23rd 1958. This simply confirmed many people's ideas of the BBC approach to jazz, and the fact that the show had continued for nearly seven years largely due to the persistence of the original producer.

All went quiet until 1993, when Jim Simpson of Big Bear Records phoned Kenny regarding the re-establishment of the Dozen, to play initially at the new Ronnie Scott's Club in Birmingham. Kenny agreed, and with a markedly different personnel from the 50's, the 90's version of the band was formed. The front page headline in the *Jazz Rag* magazine declared :

THE BOSS IS HOME – KENNY BAKER'S BOYS ARE BACK.

Jim arranged to record the last two nights which produces a new CD called *The Boss is Home* The make-up of the band now included three generations of jazz stars : Derek Healey, Bruce Adams, Simon Gardner (trumpets); Don Lusher, Bill Geldard, Richard Edwards (trombones); Roy Willox, Alan Barnes, Vic Ash, Dave Willis, Eddie Mordue (reeds); Brian Dee (piano); Dave Green (bass); Ralph Salmins (drums). Under Kenny's direction the new line-up attracted the original fans as well as a younger generation who delighted at the band's music and in particular the virtuosity and personality of the

1	Swingin' The Blues
2	Stumbling
3	Street Of Dreams
4	Slightly Latin
5	What Am I Here For?
6	Threesome
7	When Sunny Gets Blue
8	Squatty Roo
9	Golden Cress
10	Sorta' Ragtime
11	The Boss Is Home
12	More Than You Know
13	Harlem Airshaft
14	I'ts Alright With Me
15	In A Jam

BIG BEAR RECORDS,
ESS CD 224

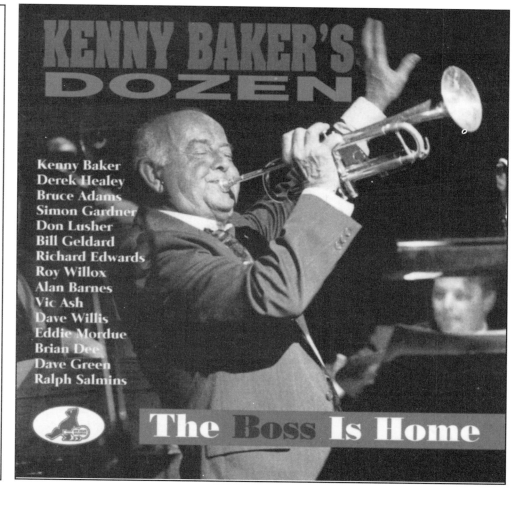

leader. An award winning CD also showed that the music style could still attract jazz lovers. The band still suffered from the problems of the economics of size, and apart from occasional concerts and broadcasts, did little more. The 'Best of British Jazz' was now going strong, and had a mix of some of the country's finest instrumentalists.

Award winning CD from Big Bear Records.

THE KENNY BAKER QUARTET
rehearsing for its debut in
Manchester August 23 1953.
(LtoR)
Cliff Ball (bass),
Stan Tracey (piano),
Kenny Baker (trumpet),
Don Lawson (drums).

Although the Dozen was taking up much of Kenny's time with the weekly broadcasts, he was developing a 'commercial' side to his playing as he was being pressed into variety performances. This meant a departure from the jazz of the Dozen to the sweet and virtuoso playing that the music halls and TV were demanding. Harry James was setting the scene in the USA with such numbers as the 'Carnival of Venice' and 'Ciribiribin'. Kenny and Eddie Calvert introduced British audiences in the country's variety theatres to this developing 'pop' music. Kenny describes this period of his career as the schizophrenic Baker, who was playing main stream jazz, pop music, and the bebop and modern jazz sounds that were drifting across the Atlantic. The end of the early Dozen meant that as well as the variety hall work, he was also able to accept the many calls for a quality musician for session work. This could be for TV background music, for playing with the re-formed Ted Heath band, under his friend and colleague Don Lusher, or for accompanying visiting American musicians, who were now beginning to visit Britain as the musicians' ban was lifted.

Add to this the resurgence of the trad music in which Britain was taking a world lead, and we can realise that there was an embarrassment of riches available to a grateful public. Kenny Baker played them all, without featuring any to the exclusion of others. In spite of the pressures of commercial music making – or perhaps because of them – Kenny was always anxious to wander into clubs where musicians were playing for their own enjoyment. One of these was the Studio Club just off Piccadilly, a club set up in 1915 by Augustus John among others, for the artistic intellectuals of the day. By the 50's, the club had added the pianist Alan Clare, who was then joined by bass player Jack Fallon, and thereafter, the evening was enhanced by who-

THE KENNY BAKER QUARTET
with singer Ruby Murray
prepares for the grand
tour of the variety halls.
(LtoR)
Stan Tracey (piano),
Kenny Baker (trumpet)
Don Lawson (drums),
Cliff Ball (bass).

ever dropped in. Humph, Wally Fawkes, Ian Christie, Johnny Dankworth and of course Kenny Baker were all there from time to time.

They were playing to one another instead of an audience shouting requests. As Kenny said at the time : "There's a lot of strain playing for people who know me. They always expect me to finish on a top G and are watching out for faults from the great man. But at this club I can play how and what I like, and if I do make a mistake, I don't have to worry." To patrons on the tiny dance floor he was just another member of the band.

Although in the early days he was accompanied by the pit orchestra while on tour, he decided that there would be a lot of sense in having his own backing group, and so in 1953 the Kenny Baker Quartet was formed. This comprised Stan Tracey on piano, Cliff Ball on bass, and Don Lawson on drums, and occasionally they were joined by 18 year old singer Ruby Murray.

Something which tells us a bit about the often hilarious life for musicians in the fifties was Don Lawson remembering sharing the bill with Kenny Graham and his Afrocubists, and the journey home without their own transport. 'The whole band went home on a London Transport trolleybus, with double bass, drums, congas, trumpet and sax, all upstairs of course.'

Work over, an interesting assortment of jazzers get together in the Studio Club.
(LtoR)
Johnny Dankworth,
Kenny Baker,
Keith Christie,
Alan Clare.

PHOTO IAN CHRISTIE

Finale to the
TEDDY WILSON CONCERT.
(LtoR)
Teddy Wilson,
Sid Phillips,
Keith Christie,
Kenny Baker,
Johnny Dankworth,
Lennie Hastings, and
Ken Ingerfield.

THE NEW MUSICAL EXPRESS

Even allowing for changes in the value of currency, it still seems a good evening out for 3/6 (about 17p) !
Advert *New Musical Express.*

A highlight for the quartet was when it was selected to to be one of the groups touring with the American piano virtuoso Teddy Wilson. A major concert was at the Royal Albert Hall, with other bands which included Freddy Randall and his Allstars, Harry Gold and his Pieces of Eight, and Basil Kirchin and his Orchestra. As part of his nationwide tour which was rapidly fully booked, an extra Teddy Wilson concert was fitted in at the Walthamstow Town Hall, and Freddie Randall expected to play with his band. Unfortunately there was a serious coach crash between Glasgow and Inverness, and several of the band were injured. A new front line was hastily put together, and Teddy Wilson found himself surrounded by some of the UK's best jazz musicians who had rushed forward to help. Kenny was on trumpet, Johnny Dankworth on alto sax, Sid Phillips on clarinet, and Keith Christie on trombone. Quite a line-up, appreciated by the audience as well as Teddy Wilson. In spite of certain Union rules about visiting Americans having to play solo, there was a great finale to the concert when the British musicians came on stage accompanied by the injured Betty Smith on tenor, and with Teddy gave a belting performance of 'One O'clock Jump' followed as an encore with 'How High the Moon'. What a night!

One digression in 1960 was a proposal from producer Ben Churchill to produce more jazz on television, and he asked Kenny to direct the new show to be entitled *Steamboat Shuffle*. The idea was to recapture the feeling of the River Boat Shuffles that had run from Richmond to Tower Bridge in the early fifties, and a 100 feet long Mississippi style paddle boat with two smoke stacks was commissioned and launched under the name Cotton-tail. The designer, Bob Fuest, claimed that it would be difficult to distinguish it from the genuine article but some doubts were expressed regarding its seaworthiness. But its success as a vehicle for the new programme was certain.

Kenny Baker and the Swamplanders from TV's STEAMBOAT SHUFFLE.

Music in the Dixieland style was to be headed by Kenny Baker's 'Swamplanders', and these were to be augmented by various of the current trad bands. When we realise that the first bands to perform alongside Kenny's were the Alex Welsh Band and the Mike Daniels Delta Jazz Band we can understand that ATV were likely to be on a winner, and so it proved. Each week there were to be visiting artists, and the first show had Cy Grant as guest, with other vocals being taken by Kenny Lynch, Peter Elliot and Joanne Scoon. The *Melody Maker* of August 13th had this to say about the launch programme :

> *This first 'Steamboat Shuffle' made a promising start, says Tony Brown. Visually interesting with camera-men making the most of the wide open spaces, – and musically varying between lively and excellent.*
>
> *The contrast between the Mike Daniels and the Alex Welsh groups brought neither discredit ... both are worth a second hearing. But the Baker crew with Kenny in formidable form, rather stole the show. Excellent arrangements played with verve, and the whole precisely integrated.'*

The show continued to involve the best of the current jazz scene, and participating bands included those of Humphrey Lyttleton, Sandy Brown and Al Fairweather, Bob Wallis, Acker Bilk, and Kenny Ball. It was hardly surprising then that the programme went from its planned four screenings to ten.

TV TIMES JULY 29TH 1960

D OWN by the River Thames, at the ABC Studios, is a dream boat that, in *Steamboat Shuffle* starting next Saturday, will strike sentimental chords in the hearts of all viewers who love Dixieland jazz of the kind featured on Mississippi paddle steamers in the early 1900s.

To present the music in a picturesque and authentic setting the show has re-created a Mississippi riverboat, nearly 100ft long, which looks so real that it might even fool an old-time riverboat captain.

For the next four Saturday evenings viewers will see the boat, named Cotton Tail, play host to a host of top jazzmen.

A specially-formed band, the Swamplanders, will appear each week led by trumpet star Kenny Baker. Other bands to be seen during the series include Humphrey Lyttelton, Mr Acker Bilk, Alex Welsh, Kenny Ball, Mike Daniels, the Al Fairweather and Sandy Brown All Stars, and the Bob Wallis Storyville Jazzmen.

Peter Elliott (often seen as a swinging ballad singer in *Oh Boy!*) is the resident vocalist. Among the scheduled guests are Cy Grant, Chas MacDevitt and Shirley Douglas, Dickie Pride, Don Rennie, Joanne Scoon, Kenny Lynch, Maggie Fitzgibbon, Marion Williams, Elaine Delmar, and Doreen Beatty.

"Some of these singers are not normally associated with jazz," director Ben Churchill told me, "but they enjoy singing it whenever they get the opportunity—and they are going to get it on this show.

"We'll provide them with various types of accompaniment, not all Dixieland. And for at least one vocal I'm going to use solo guitar accompaniment by Fitzroy Coleman. He's a fantastic player who has been rather buried in Calypso groups."

STEAMBOAT SHUFFLE - ON THE THAMES

Mr Acker Bilk and his Dixieland band

Of the bands, Churchill said: "Kenny Baker's 11-piece Swamplanders are designed to have as broad a musical appeal as possible within the field of jazz.

"We'll have a band at both ends of the boat and there will be some movement between the bands. For example, Humphrey Lyttelton will play a duet with Kenny, and the Alex Welsh band's trombonist will have a musical battle with the Swamplanders' trombonist.

"The programme will not attempt to fit everything into a period format,"

Churchill continued. "The feeling we want to create is that the musicians have found an old riverboat, have painted it up and are playing on it for their enjoyment with no attempt to make a formal TV show."

Why are riverboats regarded with such affection by jazz enthusiasts?

From the early 1900s, jazz of the type that eventually became known as Dixieland, was created by Negroes whose African rhythmic and melodic heritage was merged with the European brass band and church music traditions.

The birthplace of this new style of music-making was the Mississippi delta around New Orleans and it was the bands on pleasure steamers plying up-river from New Orleans which first popularised jazz.

So the jazz in *Steamboat Shuffle* owes its popularity in large measure to the sort of riverboat that forms the centrepiece of the show.

David Griffiths

CHAPTER 6

THE STROLLING PLAYER
From Blackpool to the London Palladium

APPEARING AS A SOLOIST in variety or with his small group, led to a different lifestyle and venues, ranging from small clubs to such as that most famous of venues – the Central Pier at Blackpool. In 1955 he landed a twenty week contract there, and like most of his bookings, this was extended so that over a four year period he appeared with a host of well known artists. 'Blackpool always had something good up its sleeve for me.' He had first played there with the Ted Heath Orchestra in 1946, when that band was making its bid for fame during the summer season. After this he was a regular visitor, first with repeated visits by the Heath band and then as a solo artist, with numerous concerts at the Opera House and the Palace Theatre.

His first major season was in 1955 with those two young men, Morecambe and Wise, and his name and theirs were truly up in lights at the Central Pier. He appeared primarily with his own back-up trio, with Johnny Flanagan on drums, Alan MacDonald on bass and Dave Milne on piano. His

'One of the nicest guys you could work with'. Kenny relaxes with Ernie Wise.

Double billed with Morecambe and Wise had to be a good start at Blackpool's Central Pier.

PHOTO H.A. HALLAS

The dapper Kenny escorts singer Joan Reagan to the Central Pier.

agent pointed out that sweet solos of the style used by Eddie Calvert – a trumpeter who Kenny had always admired – were becoming increasingly popular. Kenny agreed, and would entrance the audience with solo performances of such as 'Carnival of Venice'. It was no surprise that he was invited back. During this period he was to meet so many of the future stars of television, as the word 'variety' meant just that. Ken Dodd was an amateur trumpet player, and Kenny has said that he was one of the best comics, with the proviso that once on stage you could not stop him. Other artists would wait their turn in the wings, while Ken Dodd just kept going. The very young Petula Clark was also on the bill, and Tommy Cooper, Jewel and Wariss, singer David Whitfield and veteran Jimmy James with his young protege Roy Castle, were a few of the names that were in Blackpool, Glasgow or one of the major London theatres through the days of music hall and variety.

BLACKPOOL PANORAMA.
The Empress Ballroom
was another venue where
the Heath Band drew
huge crowds. The picture
speaks for itself.

**Ken Dodd,
but Kenny's trumpet.**

**A twenty week season
has to be better than the old days of one night stands.
Kenny arrives under the shadow of the Blackpool Tower in 1955
for his first long stay – but not his last!**

Not bad value for 4/-!
(20p in today's money)

And this was the show
you got for your 4/-.

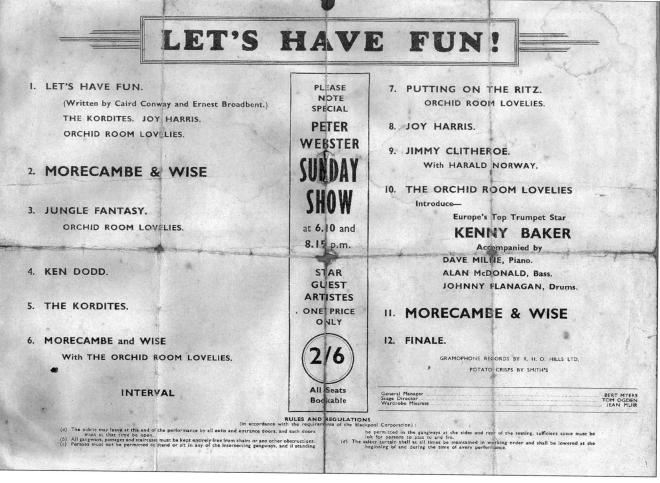

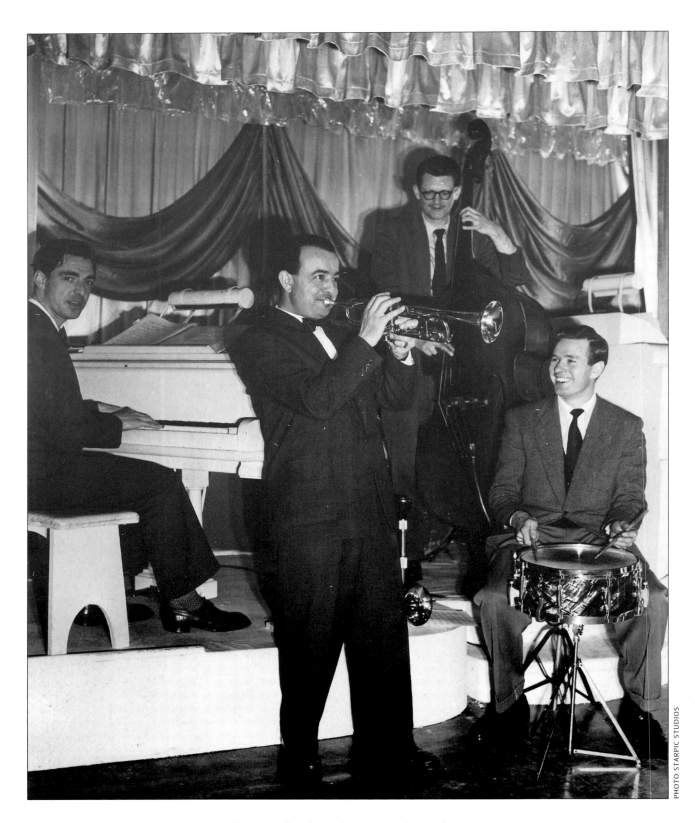

Kenny's solos always brought the house down.
When Harry James died, virtuoso Kenny was asked to take his place
in the Harry James Orchestra in California. He refused.

Another young man making his name in the jazz world, via the variety theatre, was jazz singer George Melly, who even in those days was a highly colourful character. One newspaper was predicting that 'here was a new comedy duo, with trumpeter Kenny Baker and singer George Melly', when they duetted in 'Empty Bed Blues'. George used the words, and Kenny 'acted' the part with growl trumpet. 'This is the kind of authentic comedy which truly belongs to jazz, and has nothing to do with red nose and paper balls'. George was appearing on tour with Mick Mulligan and his Magnolia Jazz Band, a lively mixture to put it mildly. The mixture was to be repeated with support of all things from the *Daily Express* who organised *Rhythm With The Stars*, a show involving British jazzers of the day.

A near disaster occurred when the BBC arrived to feature Kenny, among others, for the TV programme *Stars At Blackpool*. A few hours before the show he had to call a doctor when one of his eyelids swelled up like a balloon, and a cyst had to be removed immediately. In spite of this, the show went on, and the only concession Kenny made was to change his opening number from the theme from his radio show *Let's Settle For Music*, to the the more appropriate 'Cherry Pink' - it was in tone with his facial colour scheme!

LOOK! THE MOST COSTLY LIPS OF THEM ALL

A MAN who has insured his lips for £25,000 will play in the Daily Express music show "Rhythm with the Stars."

He is ace trumpeter Kenny Baker, acclaimed as the greatest jazz man in the country.

Kenny, equally at home with modern and traditional jazz will "blow" with both the Kirchin Band and the Mick Mulligan band.

Other star names on the bill: Eve Boswell, the Kentones, Dill Jones, Janie Marden, the Hedley Ward Trio, Ronnie Scott and George Melly.

George Melly and Kenny in action – 'a new comedy duo?'

PHOTO DAILY HERALD

**COMICS UNITED
FOOTBALL TEAM**
**First (and only) appearance
at the Grand Order of Water
Rats' Charity Match.
The team included :
(front row LtoR)
Eric Morecambe, Kenny Baker,
Stanley Matthews (referee),
Ben Wariss,
Jimmy Jewel's son Kerry.
(back row LtoR)
Jeeves, Ernie Wise,
Stan Stennett, Tommy Cooper,
Jimmy Jewel, Charlie Chester.**

Typical of his zest for life was his involvement with an amazing football team from artists in the Blackpool season playing for charity. This included Morecambe and Wise, Tommy Cooper, Bob Monkhouse, Ken Dodd, Charlie Chester, Jewel and Wariss, and Stan Stennet, and of course Kenny, playing for Comics United against Blackpool Colts, refereed by the famous Stanley Matthews. As a great afternoon out for variety fans and football fanatics, it was a winner, but as a fund raiser for the Grand Order of Water Rats charities, it raised some £1,400 in front of an audience of 10,000. Tommy Cooper strung a line of washing across the goal posts, four players brought a card table on to the pitch, the Comics made up the rules, and their team had around fifteen players when the final whistle was blown! The score was 4-4 at half time, but nobody was able to keep score after that. This was a typical way for Kenny to become involved in charity work, something he does to this day.

He was also partner for the veteran of radio and stage Vic Oliver, when they played at a Blackpool Bowls Club as a fund raiser. To this non-musical activity has to be added the fact that it was during the Blackpool seasons that he acquired his passion for golf. The all-round man was becoming fully in evidence.

PHOTO H.A. HALLAS

Blackpool residents had some reason to worry as Kenny took up golf – to be continued whenever he got the opportunity.

PHOTO BLACKPOOL GAZETTE & HERALD

BLACKPOOL BOWLS CLUB
Mr 'Show-business' (Vic Oliver) bowling, watched by Kenny (standing left) in a charity match in Blackpool. Both were well known for giving up their time for fund raising for a whole variety of good causes.

Blackpool was 'show business' in the 50's. Maybe we had TV, but they still flocked in their thousands for this sort of line-up.

THE GREAT STAR LINE-UP
At the Record Mirror's Cocktail Party at Blackpool's Norbreak Hydro Hotel 1957.

(front row LtoR)
ERNIE WISE, ALBERT BURDON, JIMMY CLITHEROE, KENNY BAKER, BEN WARRISS, JOAN TURNER and TOMMY STEELE.
(second row, seated, LtoR)
DENNY WILLIS, JIMMY JEWEL, WALLY HARPER, JOAN SAVAGE AND ROBERT EARL.
(third row LtoR)
NIRSKA, YANA, FRANCES TANNER, LENNY THE LION (being held by TERRY HALL) and STELLA TANNER.

Standing, extreme left (LtoR)
HOLGER and DOLORES, TOMMY COOPER, STAN STENNETT, ANNE SHELTON, ROY LANSFORD, KEN MORRIS.

The three young men grouped together are members of the FOUR JONES BOYS singing team and immediately behind them is BERNIE WINTERS, RUBY MURRAY, KAREN GREER, NORRIE PARAMOR, (partly hidden), BOB MONKHOUSE, DENNIS GOODWIN and BARRY HAMILTON (of The Three Deuces).

Standing between Anne Shelton and Roy Lansford is RAY MARLOWE (also of The Three Deuces)
and the face between Ruby Murray and Karen Greer belongs to the fourth famous member of the Jones Boys.

The gentleman at the back between Bob Monkhouse and Dennis Goodwin is LARRY PARNES, manager of Tommy Steele.

Weeks of living out of suitcases were beginning to pall, and Kenny decided that studio sessions based in London provided the variety of work, a good income, and the ability to be at home at nights. He was kept very busy by the BBC, providing music, usually in the Paris Cinema off Piccadilly or television work at the Studios in Shepherd's Bush. Programmes include *Round The Horne, The Generation Game, The Kenneth Williams Cabaret* and, unusually, a jazz programme with American jazz legend Art Pepper, Kenny on trumpet, and classical horn player Dennis Brain. This was typical of the originality of producer Pat Dixon.

The job was quite wearing at times. The Orchid Room Lovelies take a lesson from England's finest trumpet player.

PHOTO H.A. HALLAS

This was an exciting time, and Kenny made two steps to a more ordered life, when he bought a house in North Harrow and then married Sue. Radio, television and recordings were keeping him very busy, whether accompanying pop stars, or something as different as playing jazz to poetry read by poet laureate John Betjeman. He was able to meet up again with an old friend, when Tommy McQuater suggested he join the Jack Parnell Orchestra,

PHOTO DAILY EXPRESSS

and many happy hours were spent in TV studios with one of the most important bands of the day. Around this time he also worked with Harry Rabbinowitz and Robert Farnon, and something which continues to this day – he has a place among five trumpeters in the massive Laurie Johnson Orchestra. Not surprisingly, he was Laurie's first choice for the trumpet section and he thoroughly enjoys the novelty of working with an unusual line-up of six trumpets, four french horns, harp, five trombones, six saxes, and rhythm section. It was a sell-out at the Barbican and as *Crescendo Magazine* enthused :

> *La crème de la crème of our top music men, miraculously corralled by Laurie Johnson : exquisitely served by his brilliant orchestrations, resulting in performances of incredible polish and verve.*

The concert was captured on Horatio Nelson Video 4001.

Daily Express contribution to jazz. Mick Mulligan, (left) singer Janie Marden and Kenny prior to a week's tour of the north of England.

THE LONDON PALLADIUM MONDAY, MARCH 19th 1956 for two weeks.

The London Palladium occupies the site of the former residence of the Duke of Argyll and Earl of Aberdeen.
In 1871-86, the reconstructed building housed the famous Hengler's Circus.
The present building completed in 1910 and named The London Palladium played all the great music hall names of the day.
It later became a cinema but reverted to a variety theatre in September, 1928.

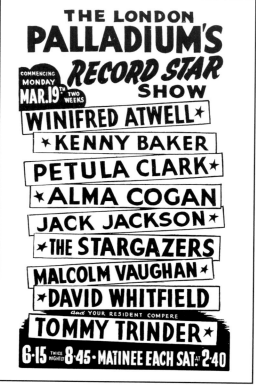

A typical variety show with many familiar names.

**A happy trumpet section
in Jack Parnell's Orchestra in
ATV Studios.
(L to R)
Derek Healey, Kenny,
Tommy McQuater, and
Bert Ezzard.**

Music For Pleasure LP 50302 1976

Side One
1 The Kiss
2 South Rampart Street Parade
3 In A Sentimental Mood
4 Trumpet Blues and Cantabile
5 Hot Toddy
6 Manhattan Spiritual
7 St. Louis Blues March

Side Two
1 Tuxedo Junction
2 Darktown Poker Club
3 Take The 'A' Train
4 Big Noise From Winnetka
5 Skin Deep
6 The Kiss

CHAPTER 7

STAGE AND SCREEN
Backstage with Vivien Leigh, Hammer Films and the Muppets

A S ONE OF THE country's leading Session musicians, Kenny was never short of somewhat unusual bookings. In 1952 he spent many weeks, evenings and matinees, sitting in a dressing room backstage at the Aldwych Theatre in London. He was accompanied by pianist Norman Stenfalt and they provided live music for Tennessee Williams' *A Streetcar named Desire*. The star was Vivien Leigh, the play was directed by Laurence

ALDWYCH THEATRE
Aldwych · W.C.2
Managing Director - - - PRINCE LITTLER
Licensed by the Lord Chamberlain to D. A. ABRAHAMS
General Manager - - - FREDERICK CARTER

VIVIEN LEIGH
IN
A STREETCAR NAMED DESIRE
by
TENNESSEE WILLIAMS
with
RENEE ASHERSON
and
BONAR COLLEANO
Directed by
LAURENCE OLIVIER
from the New York production.

THERE IS NO CHARGE FOR THIS PROGRAMME

Programme for 'A Streetcar Named Desire', a Laurence Olivier and Vivien Leigh hit of the fifties. Kenny's role was to sit in the dressing room and play 'appropriate music' which was piped onto stage as and when required.

Olivier, and the music was required from time to time to give atmosphere to the play which was based in New Orleans. The music was piped through to the auditorium. No doubt today this would be done by tape recording, but it says something for the arrangements at that time, that either the Unions would not permit it, or the taping scene was not as reliable as today.

The music was largely improvised, consisting of blues and well known

The pit orchestra of Kenny Baker and pianist Norman Stenfalt play from the backstage dressing room.

tunes of the day. The set-up must have reminded Kenny of his mother's experiences when playing music for the silent movies back in the twenties. Kenny too had to respond to the flashing signals 'get ready' and 'play'. Some breaks were five minutes and one of around twenty minutes. The latter gave enough time for a quick visit to the pub, and on more than one occasion the signal came on to an empty dressing room. The stage manager noticed, even if the audience was unaware.

Theatre-goers of the time were familiar with 'credits' that appeared on most West End programmes, – 'Stockings by Kayser Bondor', and 'Cigarettes by Abdulla'. In this case the more daring credit stated 'Miss Vivien Leigh's underwear by Daphne', and included the line 'All other clothes by Marks and Spencer'.

For Kenny it was a great opportunity to work alongside the greatest

ALDWYCH THEATRE

TENNENT PRODUCTIONS, LTD.

(in association with The Arts Council of Great Britain)

and with **IRENE MAYER SELZNICK**

present

"A STREETCAR NAMED DESIRE"

By TENNESSEE WILLIAMS

Characters in order of their appearance :

Negro Woman	BRUCE HOWARD
Eunice Hubbel...	EILEEN DALE
Stanley Kowalski	BONAR COLLEANO
Harold Mitchell (Mitch)	BERNARD BRADEN
Stella Kowalski	RENEE ASHERSON
Steve Hubbel	LYN EVANS
Blanche Du Bois	VIVIEN LEIGH
Pablo Gonzales	THEODORE BIKEL
A Young Collector	JOHN FORREST
Mexican Woman	EILEEN WAY
A Strange Woman	MONA LILIAN
A Strange Man	SIDNEY MONCKTON

Directed by **LAURENCE OLIVIER**
from the New York production

Music from the New York production with arrangements by
Leslie Bridgewater

Trumpet : Kenny Baker   Piano : Norman Stenfalt

Scenery painted by Alick Johnstone ; built by Brunskill & Loveday. Miss Vivien Leigh's costumes by Elizabeth Curzon. Miss Vivien Leigh's underwear by Daphne. Miss Vivien Leigh's shoes by Rayne.. All other ladies' clothes by Marks & Spencer. Men's clothes by M. Berman, Ltd. Properties by Robinson Bros. Furniture by The Old Times Furnishing Co. Special drapes by John Holliday & Sons, Ltd. Additional electrical equipment by The Strand Electric & Engineering Co., Ltd. Sound equipment by Bishop Sound & Electrical Co., Ltd. Lighters by Ronson Cigarettes by Abdulla.

'Who was who' at the Aldwych Theatre, London.

Kenny sat in for a late night session with the Jack Nathan band at the Coconut Grove each evening, after playing for the Aldwych Theatre play 'A Streetcar named Desire'.

actors of the day. The lead part was so stressful for Vivien Leigh (the play had her being carried off at the end in a strait-jacket), that the Monday performances were cancelled in order to give her a chance to recover. This gave Kenny the chance to do more freelance work, and this was made easy by a chance to play nightly with the Jack Nathan band at the Coconut Grove Club, where the action started at 11pm, well after the play had finished. A dash across London, into a dinner jacket, and another gig started. Ronnie Scott was in this band as was Wally Stott, who later was to give up playing, and take up writing and arranging in the

Trumpeter Kay's music is silent

With the air of a professional, film star Kay Kendall raises the trumpet to her lips. The Technicolor cameras record the scene— " a night-club "—in Pinewood Film Studios. But not a note is played. In the finished film—" Genevieve " —the music heard will be that supplied by trumpeter Kenny Baker.

PHOTO THE SCOTTISH DAILY MAIL NOVEMBER 19TH 1952

The famous scene from GENEVIEVE when Kay Kendall plays a wild trumpet after a few too many.

United States. Ronnie was also to become well known for his jazz clubs in London and Birmingham.

As though he did not have enough to occupy him, Kenny was then asked by Robert Farnon to join a forty piece band that played a regular radio series on Sundays, so there was not a lot of spare time in the week. Freelance work certainly paid the bills, and there was not much chance of getting bored. Apart from sheer stamina, the musician in this sort of life style had to be able to step in at no notice into someone else's shoes, or to be able to read at sight the arrangement put in front of him as he sat down to play. This the true professional could do, and Kenny's reputation meant that he did not need an agent, just a telephone. When asked at the time whether he found all the blowing a strain he replied in typical Baker fashion 'No, I always feel much fitter after a good session of blowing me bugle'.

The first major film he was involved with was in Shepperton Studios' *London Town*, where he and the band played some of the background music. For the musicians it meant a lot of sitting around as they made, remade and again remade the film music. For playing lots of cards and exchanging innumerable jokes, the band was rewarded with regular visits from the paymaster, lovingly referred to as 'Mr Minto', as the money he brought was always in freshly minted notes. The film was no great success, in spite of the appearance of future stars, Kay Kendall and the fifteen year old Petula Clark. It was at this time he played background music for the famous ballet film *The Red Shoes* starring Moira Shearer.

The film *Genevieve* was a huge box office success in 1952, and most people remember the scene where the delightful Kay Kendall had too much to drink in a nightclub. She took over the leader's trumpet and to everyone's amazement, and the embarrassment of boy friend played by Kenneth More, she played a hot solo before finally collapsing. The solo needless to say was played off-set by Kenny, who simply recorded what they required in a couple of hours, and went off with his fee of around £35. His brief was to play the Genevieve theme tune, then jazz it up, and finish on a top 'F'. He has still not quite forgiven the makers who omitted him from the credits, although the scene was undoubtedly one of the highlights of the film.

The main music in the film was written and played by harmonica player Larry Adler, who was told at the end of film-making that there was no money left to pay him, but would a share of any takings do? He had to agree, and the success of the film has kept the royalties coming to this day! It was only after the film was completed that Kenny found that Kay had been born in his home town of Withernsea, and that they had probably been at primary school together!

A similar scenario to *Genevieve* was enacted in Norman Wisdom's film *Trouble In Store*. Here again Norman's brilliant trumpet playing was the work of backstage Kenny Baker, just one more of the many off stage contributions made by Kenny over the years.

In the early fifties producer Michael Carreras had ben making a series of short musical films involving British bands of the day, and Kenny was often called in to play one of his virtuoso solos. In the film 'Pipes of Pan' with the Eric Winstone Band, Kenny was spotlighted amidst two bands, the Winstone band and the Studio Strings. It seemed that when a trumpet player was called for, Kenny's name was right to the fore.

Blowing other people's trumpets was to become a regular item. In 1953 Hammer films set out to produce *Trumpet Story*. Producer Michael Carreras had decided to depart from his series of short films, and to make a full scale murder mystery. American film star Alex Nicol was the trumpet player suspected of murder after topping the bill at the London Palladium. Kenny taught him the necessary actions, dubbed all the sound and then used the augmented 'Dozen' throughout the film. Realism of the trumpet playing was achieved by Kenny recording the solo, and then standing out of camera shot in front of Alex Nicol, who copied the actions closely during replay. The subsequent time delay between his fingers and the actual music was

Kenny recording with Roy Marsh on vibes.

PHOTO JOHN JAY

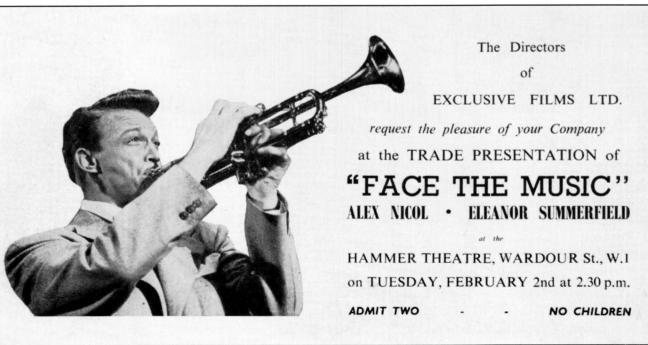

Hammer Films announce their new release.

PHOTO JOHN JAY

(opposite, top)
American actor Alex Nicol pays close attention as Kenny shows him how it is done. Pianist Stan Tracey, bass player Joe Mudell and producer Michael Carreras with trumpet.

(above)
Kenny Baker acts as conductor as actor Alex Nicol mimes his solo at the London Palladium. Musicians included the augmented 'Dozen'.

overcome by the sound track being adjusted later to bring them together. In one scene Kenny appears unusually on screen as the 'conductor' of the fifteen piece band as Nicol 'hits' the high notes on stage at the Palladium.

By the time the film was released it's title had been changed to *Face the Music*, but in spite of Kenny's playing it did not get an Oscar. Kenny's drummer Don Lawson reckoned that the plot was incomprehensible after one viewing, and at £5 for an 8am until 5pm day, nobody made a fortune, even if the drummer did get an extra 10 shillings a day for 'porterage'. It would have been reasonable to pay Kenny for three jobs at once. He coached the 'star' who really looked as though he was playing, conducted the band, and ghosted the trumpet solos, all at the same time (or so it seemed). It was a relief when the film makers changed the original title from what was to be *Songs of the Dead* which would hardly have drawn the crowds!

Four famous trumpeters meet via The Muppets. Dizzie Gillespie in 1981, Tommy McQuater on the right, and a sad looking Gonzo front centre.

An exciting involvement with television for which he has very pleasant memories, was when Jim Henson introduced *The Muppets* to a grateful nation. Kenny spent many a happy hour recording the theme music and also accompanying the amazing line-up of stars who appeared over the years. Most fun was had when each week another strange sound had to be made for the unfortunate Gonzo, the Muppet trumpeter. Needless to say Kenny was the man to produce the strangulated trumpet sound representing that week's disastrous effort by the unhappy Gonzo. He would try a variety of non standard noises until Jim said 'that's it!' and that was recorded for posterity. The musicians would arrive in the morning and receive their instructions from Jim, and after sufficient experimenting would record the background for whatever was required. This could range from a nightmare explosive cantata to the sound of baby rabbits playing glockenspiels. The band would then go home at lunch time, leaving the puppeteers to fit the actions to the music in the rest of the week.

Another involvement with television came about when Yorkshire Television produced a series, featuring James Bolam and Barbara Flynn, around titles varying from *The Beiderbecke Affair*, to *The Beiderbecke Tapes* to *The Beiderbecke Collection*. These were written by Alan Plater, and the background music centred round the leading man's love of the music of Twenty's jazz trumpeter Bix (Bismarck) Beiderbecke. The obvious choice for providing the music was Kenny, and he was accompanied by a hand-chosen array of the best British jazzers. For many viewers this must have been their first introduction to the music of someone who had made his name in a short, but lively career, when his fame as a young man had led to too much doubtful liquor brewed in the back streets of Chicago during Prohibition. Kenny is one of the many trumpeters who consider that technically and musically, Bix could have become a challenge to Louis Armstrong, had he not died aged 28 after a short professional career. Fortunately for us,

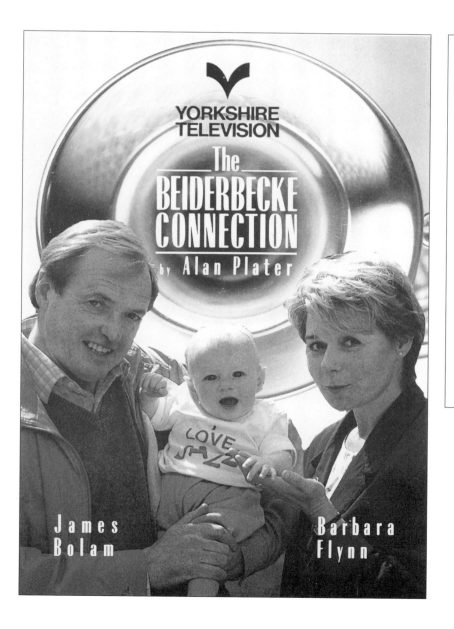

THE BEIDERBECKE CONNECTION
with
DUDLEY SUTTON, DOMINIC JEPHCOTT,
KEITH SMITH, TERENCE RIGBY,
GEORGE COSTIGAN, SEAN SCANLAN and
JUDY BROOKE
Producer: MICHAEL GLYNN
Executive Producer: KEITH RICHARDSON
Music: FRANK RICOTTI
Soloist: KENNY BAKER
Photography: PETER JACKSON
Sound: BARRIE FOX and TERRY CAVAGIN
Editor: DAVID ASPINALL
Designer: MICHAEL LONG and
ANDREW SANDERSON
Costume: BRIAN CASTLE and JANICE MARSDEN
Production: PETER LOVER, IAN FERGUSON and
PATRICIA ROBERTSHAW
Director: ALAN BELL

Starts SUNDAY NOV 27th at 8.45pm on ITV

**For the TV production of
THE BEIDERBECKE CONNECTION
the music was skilfully composed and
arranged by Frank Ricotti in the style
of the Twenties' recordings of
jazz trumpeter Bix Beiderbecke.
The solo passages by Kenny Baker
are played with his usual
flair, taste and precision.**

**THE FRANK RICOTTI
ALL STARS**
at a Bix recording
session included
Roy Willox (C-mel sax),
Kenny (cornet),
Frank Ricotti (MD),
Don Lusher (trombone), and
Dave Willis (cl/bar sax).

it was decided to capture the music on a long playing record produced by Dormouse Records (DM 20) in 1988, and arranger (and vibes player) Frank Ricotti composed most of the music in the Bix style, and this was delivered by Kenny and his colleagues.

With this sort of experience behind him, Kenny smiles when asked why he didn't just form a big band and make his fortune that way. He refers to the huge variety of experiences the freelance can get, without the hassle of organising, arranging transport and paying a large collection of musicians. The session musician can enjoy his music, earn his money and if like Kenny, could then go to a club anonymously and play jazz just for the fun of it - or go back to Harrow or Felpham and get on with his home life.

A Bix recording session in progress.

BIX BEIDERBECKE
(1903-31)
Self-taught, Beiderbecke
was the first white soloist in
jazz to gain the admiration
of black musicians.
He made his name with
various small jazz groups,
such as the Wolverines, and
later spent much of his time
with commercial bands such
as Paul Whiteman.

**Kenny with author Alan Plater,
in Hull 1998 for a concert
BIX AND ALL THAT JAZZ.**

Dormouse Records LP DM 20 1988

Side One

1　The Connection
2　Viva Le Van
3　Morgan's Mystery
4　First Borns Lullaby
5　Tulips for Chris
6　Barney's Walk
7　Boys In Blues
8　Hobson's Chase

Side Two

1　Tiger Jive
2　Scouting Ahead
3　Jennie's Tune
4　Live At The Limping Whippet
5　Russian Over
6　Dormouse Delights
7　Cryin' All Day

A STAR AMONG STARS
Bing, Satchmo, Goodman, Streisand …

I N A CAREER as long and varied as Kenny Baker's, we can rightly assume that he must have met so many of the stars of the day, whether we are thinking of the Sandy Powell of the late Thirties or singer/guitarist George Benson of the Nineties.

Initially he was part of the famous bands – Lew Stone, Jack Hylton, Ambrose, Geraldo, and Ted Heath, until he decided to go freelance. It was during this time he began to meet up with musicians who were to form part of his music making right to this day – Don Lusher and Jack Parnell . Each of these formed a big band which was to feature Kenny as lead trumpet, Jack Parnell with his own band, and likewise Don with his own band, as well as the Ted Heath band which Don took over when Ted died.

By the time Kenny was billed alongside Eartha Kitt in 1956, he had already appeared three times in Royal Command Performances.

Two of the best. Bobby Hackett exchanges notes with our own chef de trumpet.

PHOTO CRESCENDO PUBLICATIONS

Then the variety halls introduced him to everyone who became anyone in the television age just emerging – so we have the young Morecambe and Wise, Ken Dodd, Tommy Cooper, Jewell and Wariss, Charlie Chester and so on.

As session musician, he was always being called on to accompany visiting international celebrities, and here the list is endless. It includes Benny Goodman, Louis Armstrong, Billy May, Dizzie Gillespie, Bobby Hackett, Tony Bennett , Eartha Kitt, Nellie Lutcher, Bing Crosby, most of the Count Basie band, Billie Holiday and Barbra Streisand. It was clear that in those days if you were a visiting international star going to perform in the UK, 'get Kenny Baker on trumpet, Johnny Dankworth on alto, Don Lusher on trombone, and Jack Parnell on drums'. As time went by these were augmented by such as Brian Lemon on piano, Allan Ganley on drums, and a number of other session musicians, who had opted out of regular 'pit' band type commitments, to enjoy the variety of gigs that deservedly came their way.

Bing misses a four feet put.

All did not always go well, and Kenny was renowned for crossing swords with none other than Benny Goodman during a concert tour in Italy. Benny would not agree to Kenny's tempo for one of his own arrangements, so Kenny in the end played at his own speed. When the lead trumpet was a full bar behind, the famous Goodman reluctantly gave way. You don't fool with a Yorkshireman!

He worked closely with Bing Crosby at his Christmas show at ATV

Elstree, when Bing had his whole family with him. Kenny enjoyed the opportunity of talking with the great man, particularly on the subject of Bix Beiderbecke, who Bing had worked with in the very early Paul Whiteman band. It was shortly after the Christmas show that Bing was taken ill and died. Producer Pete Moore decided that it would be a better tribute to Bing if his last recording with a trio was enhanced by a full orchestra. With the marvels of technology the addition was made, and an LP produced with a big band of session musicians, including solos by Kenny Baker.

An exciting event for all British jazz musicians was the visit to the UK of Louis Armstrong in 1957, and this was highlighted by a meeting in a London restaurant with some of the music's key representatives. Louis was his usual charming self, and for Kenny it was a chance to rub shoulders with his boyhood hero. Without the early records of Louis and Duke Ellington, Kenny might well have continued along the path of brass band and classical playing which he had been taught as a young lad – which would have been a great loss to British popular music.

The photos that follow take us through many aspects of Kenny's career, and prove the point that a picture is worth a thousand words !

SURPRISE LUNCH FOR LOUIS ARMSTRONG arranged by **Humphrey Lyttleton.** (LtoR) Geraldo, Leslie 'Jiver' Hutchinson, Vic Lewis, Louis , Buddy Featherstonhaugh, Jack Parnell, Cyril Stapleton, Laurie Gold, Kenny, Ronnie Aldrich, Humph, Billy Munn.

Benny Goodman looks friendly enough –
Kenny, among many others, fell out with him.
The photograph is inscribed :
To Kenny, A really fine trumpet player –
thanks for your fine efforts.
My best, Benny.

Benny Goodman chats up
the audience at the London
Palladium. Kenny in back
row, Johnny Dankworth in
front row.

Surely every jazz band leader's dream – to accompany Billie Holiday.
'A lovely lady, and what a voice' said Kenny after the concert.
One of the rare occasions that the Dozen appeared outside a studio.

PHOTO YORKSHIRE POST

With the end of the Musicians' Union strike,
the UK began to hear some of the finest American jazz musicians.
(L to R)
Kenny Baker, Otis Stann, Muddy Waters (seated),
George Chisholm, and the Honourable Gerald Lascelles.

FROM CHEAM TO CYPRUS
Comedian Tony Hancock took
time off from Railway Cuttings to
tour British army camps in Cyprus.
Kenny provided the musical
back-up with a group including
tenor player Betty Smith.

PHOTO MELODY MAKER

Jazz fan Lord Montagu
invited the Count Basie Band
to the Motor Museum for
'tea', escorted by
Kenny Baker.
Sherry anybody?

Basie trumpeter Joe
Newman shares a ride
with Kenny in one of the
Motor Museum's exhibits.

Arranger for the famous
Paul Whiteman Orchestra,
veteran Ferde Grofe talks
with the 28-year old Kenny,
then arranging for the
Ted Heath band.

**BARBRA STREISAND …
AND OTHER MUSICAL
INSTRUMENTS**
CBS LP 69052 1973
For sheer scale, the
'Barbra Streisand
and other Musical
Instruments' album
kept Kenny's trumpet
and around 150 other
instruments busy for
a massive recording
session. The TV Special
used eight drummers
from Ghana and many
other ethnic instruments,
as well as the sounds
produced by steam kettle,
toaster, sewing machine,
electric shaver and
musical saw.

If you played in the
Jack Parnell band, you
were going to have
fun. A distinguished
brass line-up for the
Barbra Streisand
TV Special.
(LtoR)
Jack Armstrong,
Lennie Busby,
Kenny Baker,
Tommy McQuater,
Alan Aitkin.

Who's that man reading the Daily Express? Kenny passes the time at another recording session for the Barbra Streisand TV show.

Session musician was often a tiring job. Kenny takes a nap in ATV studios.

Guests with the BBC Big Band, Kenny with singer Angela Christian and music director Barry Forgie.

Billy May directs the BBC Big Band with guest soloist Kenny Baker at London's Royal Festival Hall. Billy had been trumpet player and arranger with the Glenn Miller, Bob Crosby, and Woody Herman bands, as well as working with Bing Crosby, Frank Sinatra, Ella Fitzgerald and almost all artists of similar stature.

PHOTO JOHN KNELL

Kenny and George Benson, recording for George Benson's new album with the Robert Farnon Orchestra.

Old friends, still playing, meet up at the Barbican Theatre in 1998 during a Ted Heath concert organised by Don Lusher. Kenny and George Shearing with Mrs Shearing between them. They had been making music together on and off since 1942.

PHOTO JOHNNY GR

BAND OF BANDLEADERS

– these were the men whose names were well known in the realms of British swing and dance music of the fifties. All band leaders, but not many active musicians. What were they playing? Nothing, it was a photo opportunity!

Violins : GEORGE MELACHRINO, CYRIL STAPLETON, SIDNEY LIPTON.
Piano : SID DEAN. Timpani : ERIC DELANEY. Vibes : REG WALE. Drums : GEORGE ELRICK.
Bass : BILLY TERNENT. Accordions : ERIC WINSTONE, MALCOLM LOCKYER.
Trumpets : NAT GONELLA, TONY OSBORNE, EDDIE CALVERT, KENNY BAKER.
Trombones : TED HEATH, JACK BENTLEY, WOLF PHILLIPS, PAUL FEHNOULET.
Clarinets : SID PHILLIPS, NAT TEMPLE, HARRY LEADER, HARRY ROY.
Saxophones : BOB MILLER, KEN MACINTOSH, JOHNNIE GRAY, DAVID EDE.
Leader : HARRY RABINOWICH.

CHAPTER 9

NOT ALL JAZZ

Symphony orchestras, youth orchestras, not to mention brass bands!

RAISING MONEY FOR CHARITY by playing football or bowls, was something Kenny was to extend by the more direct use of his trumpet skills. But the sheer size of some of these functions must have surprised even him, when he found himself with something the size of the London Symphony Orchestra, or the Midlands Youth Jazz Orchestra. The charities or good causes came from all directions, and he would always offer his services willingly.

As early as 1942 he took part in making a record, the takings from which were to help provide 'comforts' to be sent to a much beleaguered Merchant Navy, which was suffering terrible losses in the oceans of the world. The title 'Red Duster Rag' was written for the occasion by George Chisholm, and other young musicians giving their services, included Tommy McQuater, George Chisholm, Jack Parnell and Stephane Grappelli. The 'thank you' letter sent to Kenny is quite dramatic in its appearance and content.

THE CITY OF LIVERPOOL MERSEYSIDE POLICE BAND enjoy the solo of Kenny Baker.

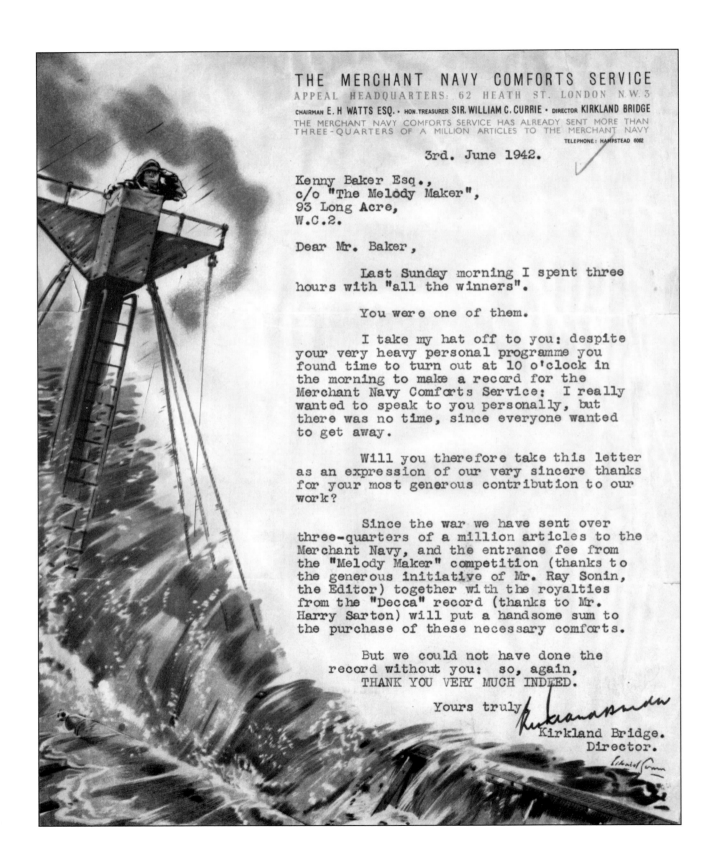

THE MERCHANT NAVY COMFORTS SERVICE
APPEAL HEADQUARTERS: 62 HEATH ST. LONDON N.W. 3
CHAIRMAN E. H WATTS ESQ. • HON. TREASURER SIR. WILLIAM C. CURRIE • DIRECTOR KIRKLAND BRIDGE
THE MERCHANT NAVY COMFORTS SERVICE HAS ALREADY SENT MORE THAN
THREE-QUARTERS OF A MILLION ARTICLES TO THE MERCHANT NAVY
TELEPHONE: HAMPSTEAD 6062

3rd. June 1942.

Kenny Baker Esq.,
c/o "The Melody Maker",
93 Long Acre,
W.C.2.

Dear Mr. Baker,

Last Sunday morning I spent three
hours with "all the winners".

You were one of them.

I take my hat off to you: despite
your very heavy personal programme you
found time to turn out at 10 o'clock in
the morning to make a record for the
Merchant Navy Comforts Service: I really
wanted to speak to you personally, but
there was no time, since everyone wanted
to get away.

Will you therefore take this letter
as an expression of our very sincere thanks
for your most generous contribution to our
work?

Since the war we have sent over
three-quarters of a million articles to the
Merchant Navy, and the entrance fee from
the "Melody Maker" competition (thanks to
the generous initiative of Mr. Ray Sonin,
the Editor) together with the royalties
from the "Decca" record (thanks to Mr.
Harry Sarton) will put a handsome sum to
the purchase of these necessary comforts.

But we could not have done the
record without you: so, again,
THANK YOU VERY MUCH INDEED.

Yours truly,

Kirkland Bridge.
Director.

One of Kenny's earliest 'thank you' letters. It speaks for itself.

In 1975 he took part in a Gala Concert in the Royal Festival Hall for the Army Benevolent Fund, and was in the distinguished company of the Band of the Kneller Hall, Royal Military School of Music. The music varied from that of Rossini and Saint-Saens to Grand Opera choruses, and amidst all the pomp and circumstance of that music, the Symphonic Suite by Bencriscutto was played by the Don Lusher Quartet with Kenny on trumpet. A huge change from accompanying Sandy Powell in the early music halls!

"Your playing was a revelation to us all, and I know the band, and particularly the youngsters, are still buzzing from the experience."

THE LEADER, CITY OF LIVERPOOL MERSEYSIDE POLICE BAND

As a contrast he caused much excitement when he played alongside the members of the City of Liverpool Merseyside Police Band. For those who had not heard him before, or who thought that a jazz man would not manage some of the technical intricacies of some brass band music, there was a wonderful surprise. In a letter of thanks the leader of those musicians said 'your playing was a revelation to us all, and I know the band, and particularly the youngsters, are still buzzing from the experience'.

Don Lawson, drummer of the original Kenny Baker Quartet, relishes the story of Kenny appearing in front of a packed Albert Hall audience at the National Brass Band Championships, when the other musicians were the finest brass players the country could provide. When Kenny first came on

Another successful play-along, this time in 1990 with Ian Darrington, Director of the Wigan Youth Jazz Orchestra. Kenny's wife Sue looks equally happy with the gig.

stage, the audience gave him a huge reception, with many of the brass players watching him with interest – who was this jazz guy? After the interval, when Kenny made his second appearance, the hard-bitten brass players cheered him to the echo – he had earlier astonished them with his rendering

The One & Only
MISTER
BILLY ECKSTINE

Compere Bob Holness President of Niners Club

Musical Director Robert Tucket

THE 'NINER CLUB' SOUVENIR PROGRAMME 1980

DUNCAN LAMONT
HENRY MACKENZIE
TOM MCQUATER
ROY WILLOX
ROY WILLIAMS

* * * * * * * * * *

JACK EMBLOW
and
JOHN McLEVY

* * * * * * * * * *

ROY SWINFIELD

* * * * * * * * * *

KENNY BAKER
DON LUSHER

* * * * * * * * * *

GEORGE CHISHOLM

* * * * * * * * * *

Piano
BILL McGUFFIE
BRIAN LEMON
NORMAN STENFALT
JOHN PEARCE

* * * * * * * * * *

Bass
LENNIE BUSH
FRANK DONNISON

* * * * * * * * * *

Drums
JACK PARNELL
BOBBY ORR

* * * * * * * * * *

The Niner Club Co-op
GEOFF RIDEOUT
SYD CLEMENTS
CO LEADERS

* * * * * * * * * *

Producer
DON SAYER

* * * * * * * * * *

'THE ONE AND ONLY
MISTER BILLY ECKSTINE'

THE 'NINER CLUB'
raises money for autistic
children supported by many of
Britain's top jazz musicians.

of the fiendishly difficult 'Carnival of Venice'. And he always illustrated what so many critics said about him : 'showing his incredible technique and musicianship, but without showing off'.

Something quite different was the concert in aid of autistic children, when some of Britain's best jazz men supported the redoubtable Billy Eckstine in a concert for the 'Niner Club'. This club was originated by the pianist Bill McGuffie for musicians who, like him, had lost one finger, hence the title 'Niners'. He was soon joined by Russ Conway and Eric Delaney, after which you could join as an ordinary member if you were missing any limb, or any other part of your body – or just wanted to help raise money for the Autistic children, who were the focus of its activities. The concert was provided by a collection of some of the top jazz and swing musicians of the day, and Billy Eckstine went home happy, having had the pleasure of the finest back-up band he could have wished for. The 'Niners' are still in action, and the Best of British Jazz continues to give its support.

Perhaps one very encouraging development has been the popularity of the massive youth jazz orchestras, now a familiar sound in many counties and cities. Kenny Baker was quick to see the value of these in giving young people a chance to hear, and play, the sort of music that was never heard in

Kenny Baker in Brass Band Festival

TRUMPET-LEADER Kenny Baker will make musical history at the Albert Hall tomorrow (Saturday) when he appears as star soloist in the *Daily Herald* Brass Band Festival Concert.

It is the first time a jazz musician has been selected to play at this traditional annual event which climaxes a countrywide contest involving about 500 bands.

Kenny is an appropriate choice, for apart from his present status in the jazz field, he began his musical career on cornet with the West Hull Silver Band at the age of 11.

Becoming interested in the trumpet, he took his first step towards ultimate fame by winning a MELODY MAKER dance-band contest as a semi-pro.

TWO FAMOUS BRASSMEN

Kenny Baker, guest soloist at the " Daily Herald " Brass Band Festival Concert at the Albert Hall last Saturday, discusses mouthpieces with famous cornettist Harry Mortimer, conductor of the winning band, Fairey Aviation. Harry has conducted the winning band at these contests eight years out of the past ten. Kenny was accompanied by his quartet.

MELODY MAKER

the ubiquitous *Top of the Pops*. The National Youth Jazz Orchestra (NYJO) soon became the dream of young musicians. Many of the others bands with a similar age group are at much the same high level, and give great pleasure to audiences around the UK. There are too many to mention here, but Kenny was to meet and accompany the luckier ones during the School Proms at the Royal Albert Hall.

In 1982 Kenny was guest at one of these proms, when he was approached by a young violinist who was to play the Mendelssohn violin concerto. 'Hello maestro, can we play some jazz?' It was Nigel Kennedy, and never one to say 'no', Kenny contacted the organiser Larry Westland, who happily agreed for an extra item. Don Lusher and a young drummer from the Doncaster Youth Jazz Orchestra were hastily briefed. A delighted audience heard an unusual version of 'Tea For Two' played by a unique quartet. The young people involved must have enjoyed the official and unofficial participation by Kenny Baker at the Royal Albert Hall.

At a concert by the East Norfolk Schools Big band, a reporter was amused to hear a teenage trumpet player say 'He's not bad, is he?' In his report for

'TEA FOR TWO'
by an unusual four.
(L to R)
Nigel Kennedy (violin),
drummer from the
Doncaster Youth Jazz
Orchestra, Kenny on cornet,
and Don Lusher provide an
unscheduled item for the
Schools Prom audience at
the Royal Albert Hall.

the local paper, he wrote: 'At a time when most men are looking forward to retirement (this was in 1985!), he delighted the audience and the youngsters with his sparkingly brilliant trumpet playing and with his generous comments. He involved the band,and after his solo items, thrilled the young musicians by sitting in with the trumpet section. We could only watch and listen in amazement as he played "How High the Moon" unaccompanied'.

THE MIDLAND YOUTH JAZZ ORCHESTRA (all forty two of them) complete with flared trousers and a proud looking Kenny Baker – this was the cover of one of their LPs.

These remarks typify the way Kenny would take part, and inject some of his own enthusiasm into the other players and the audience. He travels all over the country, and invariably leaves happy memories with yet another group of budding musicians. Perhaps Kenny's own words on the subject says it all. 'All I can say is that when I did the Schools Prom it was one of the greatest sensations I have ever experienced. What a tremendous thing it is getting all those talented young people together and opening the public's eyes. The atmosphere at a Schools Prom is unique.'

'All I can say is that when I did the Schools Prom it was one of the greatest sensations I have ever experienced. What a tremendous thing it is getting all those talented young people together and opening the public's eyes. The atmosphere at a Schools Prom is unique.'

KENNY BAKER

In my own experience I was involved with a charity function for the St Wilfrid's Hospice in Chichester. The Duke of Norfolk had given the Hospice the use of the magnificent Arundel Castle, music was to be provided by The Chichester College Big Band under its Director David Wales, and the agreement of Kenny Baker and National Award Winner Bobby Wellins to appear meant an immediate sell out of tickets. They did not just 'appear', they became part of

THE EAST NORFOLK SCHOOLS BIG BAND
augmented by one more in the trumpet section.

PHOTO PHIL CROW

the band, and brought the house down by sheer personality and professionalism. Naturally the formal music was the highlight of the evening, but not many people sitting down to supper during the interval, noticed that Kenny had left his meal. He had quietly wandered over to sit in with the local traditional jazz band that was playing throughout the meal. He really loves playing anytime, anywhere, and the George Bennett Regis Jazz Band will rarely have been in such exalted company.

HE SINGS AS WELL!
The wheel turns full circle as Kenny finds himself back with the boys in air force blue for the first time since 1945.
THE ROYAL AIR FORCE COLLEGE BAND
at Cranwell in 1998.

THE LONDON PALLADIUM
Monday, November 17th, 1980
Lord Delfont, Louis Benjamin, & Reg Swinson M.B.E.
tender their congratulations to

Kenny Baker

on being selected to appear before

HER MAJESTY QUEEN ELIZABETH
THE QUEEN MOTHER

on the occasion of the

ROYAL VARIETY PERFORMANCE

in aid of
The Entertainment Artistes' Benevolent Fund

Wednesday, 6th November 1985 at 7.45pm

Royal Gala Concert

in aid of the St. Paul's Cathedral
Choir School Foundation

in the presence of H.R.H. The Duchess of Kent

Kenny Baker, Richard Baker, Jack Brymer,
Douglas Cummings, Paul Davies, Christopher Dearnley,
Richard Hickox, Philip Jones Brass Ensemble,
King's Singers, Andrew Lucas, London Symphony Orchestra,
The Lord Mayor, St. Giles String Quartet,
Prunella Scales, John Scott, St. Paul's Cathedral Choir,
Tommy Steele, Timothy West

The St. Giles String Quartet will be playing
in the Foyer before the concert:
Schubert String Quintete in C Major for two violins,
viola and two cellos, Op. 163

Barbican Hall
The Barbican Centre is owned, funded and managed
by the Corporation of the City of London *Director: Henry Wrong*

We should like to thank the Arthur Andersen & Co Foundation for their generous support of this Concert

From the sea front at Withernsea in 1934 to the Barbican Hall in London in 1985 – and now in the most distinguished company.

In 1985, the Barbican Hall and a Royal Gala Concert had him in the company of Clarinetist Jack Brymer, guitarist Carlos Bonell and the London Symphony Orchestra in the world premiere of Tommy Steele's Portrait of Pablo Picasso. In the same concert were Richard Baker, The St Paul's Cathedral Choir, The King's Singers, Prunella Scales and Timothy West, so if we rate a man by the company he keeps…!

CHAPTER 10

AWARDS AND ACCOLADES
Over sixty years of critical acclaim

F OR SOMEONE who has been playing superbly for more than half a century, it is not surprising that the number of British national awards and glowing comments from the critics make such good reading. Even Kenny can lose track of the number of times he was voted 'Top Trumpet of the Year' by the *Melody Maker* or *The New Musical Express*. Top of the poll for eight years running means his study is lined with certificates and photos of award ceremonies. His first award for top trumpet player was in 1942, and his most recent presentation was the National Jazz Award for the best big band of 1996. Anyone who has heard the current Baker Dozen will not be surprised that they were selected. His appearances at the Royal Command Performances are among many happy memories, and we will all excuse a natural pride in being selected. Fifty four years of staying at the top, and there will, no doubt, be more accolades on the way.

An oft-repeated scene as Kenny receives yet another 'Top of the Poll' Award. On this occasion he and vibes player Tito Burns are being presented with their awards by Harry Dawson.

PHOTO KEN BROOKS

Browse through the musical press over the years, spot the Kenny Baker name, and read on. Much research has failed to find a review that has anything derogatory to say about him, as a musician or as a personality. The following collection is a selection from the *Melody Maker*, *The New Musical Express*, and some Daily papers. They need no comment.

"I feel that the solos recorded in my early days with the Buddy Featherstonehaugh Sextet and Harry Hayes and his band are among my best. They were spontaneous and full of ideas."

KENNY BAKER
WRITES IN *PLAY THAT MUSIC* EDITED BY SINCLAIR TRAILL

They (Buddy Featherstonehaugh and Kenny) dig into the piece with confidence, Kenny especially doing a good job in his usual mixture of tasteful and more flashy high note solos, but never failing to exhibit that grand control of his instrument for which he has long been renowned.

Melody Maker 1944

His records are really delightful. On both sides he plays magnificent trumpet. It is emotionally uninhibited, almost to the point of effusiveness, and it sounds none the less so because of his full luscious tone. Kenny has a sense of jazz that always saves his emotionalism from sounding cloying or insincere. Kenny's arrangements are quite a revelation in how to write in the modern manner, and yet keep the music melodious in anybody's sense of the word.

Melody Maker 1951

PHOTO IVOR RICHMAN

**(LtoR) Don Macaffer, Coleridge Good, Kenny Baker, Jack Parnell playing at the first Swing Shop Concert.
September 30th 1945, Adelphi Theatre London.**

The readers of the Melody Maker make their choice.

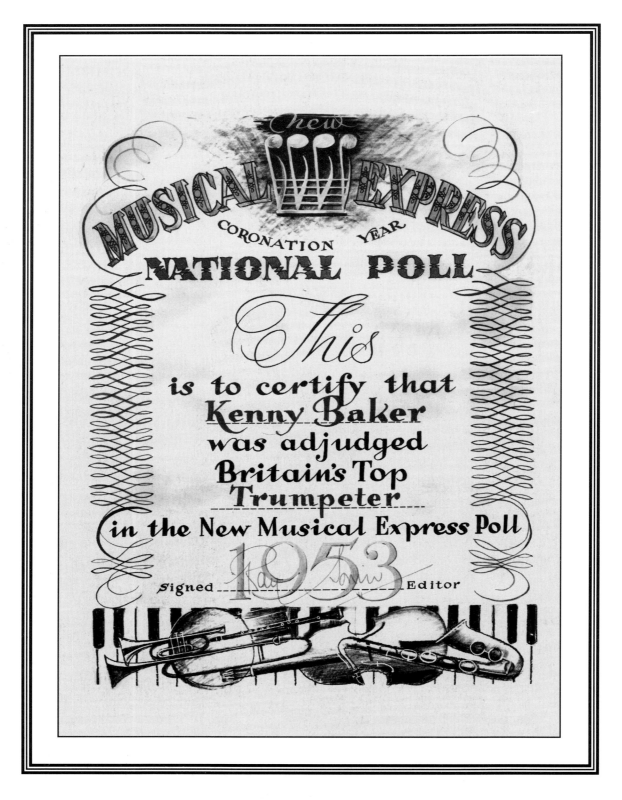

The readers of The New Musical Express make their choice.

These four sides get their four star ratings mainly of course on Kenny's playing. He has something besides those two important T's – tone and technique: he is still one of the most enterprising stylists we have. There is no one else with quite as much individuality.

Melody Maker 1952

Kenny – a really fine trumpet player – thanks for your fine efforts.

Benny Goodman after Palladium Concert 1952

KENNY BAKER **8 years running**
1-2-3-4-5-6-7-8
TOP OF THE POLL

Yet again Kenny Baker takes top place as Britain's Trumpet Star—a terrific run of successes! Congratulations Kenny!... Listen to this grand artist playing on the Light Programme every Thursday at 10.45 p.m. Note his wonderful technique; and notice how his "New Creation" Trumpet responds to whatever he demands of it.

Ask your local dealer!

always playing

THE *Besson* "NEW CREATION" TRUMPET

Good publicity for the makers of the trumpet,

'*Let's Settle for Music*' has brought back jazz-with-a-sparkle to the air; it has a wider appeal than jazz purity shows; it has none of the plodding mediocrities of most dance band programmes; it plays new and it plays old – but it always plays well. It is because of this fine example that it has been chosen by the MM's Critics as the 'Influence of the Year.'

Melody Maker 1953

TRUMPET

1	**KENNY BAKER**	4633
2	**Eddie Calvert**	3976
3	**Jimmy Deuchar**	2321
4	Bobby Pratt	1832
5	Joe Hunter	1400
6	Albert Hall	906
7	Humphrey Lyttelton	874
8	Freddy Randall	844
9	Johnny Oldfield	651
10	Stan Roderick	630
11	Freddy Clayton	623
12	Eddie Blair	617
13	Derrick Abbott	530
14	Terry Brown	347
15	Bert Courtley	268
16	Duncan Campbell	144
17	Bert Ezzard	60

**Readers of NME
(The New Musical Express)
voted for their favourite
British dance bands,
musicians and singers. The
batting list voted for
trumpet players in 1954.**

**(opposite)
Part of the The New Musical Express
voting form. Some thought had to
go into its completion!**

**KENNY BAKER,
a nineteen-fifties
publicity shot.**

THE NEW MUSICAL EXPRESS   *

MUSICAL EXPRESS AWARDS OF

(FINAL ENTRY FORM No. 4)   (Each sub-division should be marked out of 10)

STANDING MUSICIAN OF THE YEAR (Soloist on any Instrument)

INTONATION	TECHNIQUE	EXTEMPORISING	STYLE	SINCERITY	PHRASING	INDIVIDUALITY	TONE	FLUENCY

CALISTS (either with a dance band, or a recording, radio or variety soloist)   *(Do not complete if previously sent in)*

(me here)	INTONATION	INDIVIDUAL-ITY	RHYTHM	SINCERITY	STYLE	PHRASING	CONTROL	CHOICE OF SONGS	PERSONALITY

This week sees the appearance of Britain's top trumpet man, Kenny Baker, at the NME Poll-winners' Concert at the Royal Albert Hall. He joins Johnny Dankworth, Ronnie Scott, Jack Parnell, Bill McGuffie and Johnny Hawksworth.

Melody Maker 1953

But it is with great pride that I say in Kenny Baker we have here in England, one of the most accomplished trumpet players anywhere in the world. This recording is a show-case for Kenny whose brilliance transcends any shortcomings of recording.

The New Musical Express 1953

This group will play jazz hot and smooth in a manner that will bring out the virtuosity of each member. No one can doubt that Baker has the knack of creating the spirit in which good jazz is found … it is not only therefore for his polished trumpet work that he has been chosen to lead this group, but also for his ability as an arranger.

Melody Maker – 'the ideal modern group' 1954

The Kenny Baker Quartet provides excellent swing in 'The Continental / Hayfoot Strawfoot' with Kenny showing that he can swing a small group just as effectively as he does a power-house crew, without overblowing or showing off his superb technique.

Gramophone Record Review 1954

PHOTO COLIN BUSBY

**Kenny doing his solo in 'Chelsea'. This was composed in the late thirties by "Fats" Waller while on a visit to England.
The studio photo shows work in progress on The Very Best Of Ted Heath CD. A new digital recording from Horatio Nelson Records, CDSIV 6150 1995.**

Here's a gift for those who are sated with indifferent recordings of mediocre pops ... a new contract with Philips will put our number one trumpet player where he belongs – right at the top! He's been there long enough in the profession ... now Joe Public will realise his worth, if that matters to a sincere musician like Kenny. Trumpet playing *in excelsis* (and occasionally *in alt*) ... no jazz, but masterly phrasing, gorgeous tone and fabulous technique that makes all competitors look silly.

Gramophone Record Review 1954

The sound that comes from the radiogram is that of the mellow trumpet of Kenny Baker, sweet and pure, against a lush background ... and that's how my record of the week was born. It's first rate and earns this column's Oscar.

Daily Mirror 1954

British jazz is good enough to be appreciated as one of the newest expressions of an old and distinguished culture ... Ulanov singles out Heath, Dankworth, Kenny Baker, Tito Burns ... for special praise.

Metronome Year-book 1954 (American) -
Barry Ulanov Survey of British Jazz.

Kenny recording 'Tribute To The Great Trumpeters'. A new digital recording from Horatio Nelson Records, CDSIV 1124 1993.

Lennie Bush and Kenny.

PHOTOS DENNIS MATTHEWS

Geoff Young – Engineer with Kenny Baker.

PHOTO BERNARD LONG

If any doubt lingers on that Kenny Baker is 'the king' of jazz in Britain, it was banished last night in a 'Jazz Unlimited' concert at Manchester's Free Trade Hall ... Mr Baker played what was certainly the hottest trumpet in the City since America's Wild Bill Davison was on hand.

Manchester Evening Chronicle 1957

Kenny and wife Sue being presented to Princess Alexandra at a ROYAL GALA PERFORMANCE. Organiser Ken Lodge seems happy enough.

Kenny's performance leaves no room for doubt that he can ably support the claim to be Britain's best trumpet technician – in the modern field. His technical brilliance is heard at its finest in 'Africa' and 'Carnival of Venice' – his handling of a Bach fanfare trumpet both brings out the beauty of the piece's theme and demonstrates his ingenuity.

Melody Maker 1957

Kenny Baker and his Dozen in the first 6-5 Special manages the almost impossible task of bringing purist jazz to a variety hall audience. He plays in what is known as the Mainstream idiom, neither traditional nor modern , but a subtle blending of the two. And he succeeds ... he is certainly this country's greatest trumpeter of the day, and his pure drive and unbounded zest for the job, communicates to the rest of the band, producing a lively showmanship offering, that never sacrifices itself on the altar of commercialism.

London Sporting Review, 1958

'I could earn much more as a solo commercial artist playing rubbish, but I get far greater enjoyment out of playing with the Dozen' ...
Kenny in interview with Maurice Burman, critic of *Melody Maker* 1958

Britain's top trumpeter Kenny Baker has one great handicap – HE CAN'T PLAY CORN – so the disc companies almost wrote him off commercially. Now Nixa are gambling on 'Bakerloo Non-Stop' a real classy beat number. And whether it sells or not, it's my PIC OF THE DISCS for this week.
Sunday Pictorial, 1958

Bakerloo Non stop – one of Kenny's own compositions, there's nothing underground about the noise you get on this record. It's got the kind of

drive I could listen to all night – and the studio balance is first rate. This underlines the claim to be the best trumpet man we've got ... This could be his biggest seller.
Disc 1958

... I say he is one of the greatest trumpet virtuosi in the world today, and without qualification, the greatest trumpet man Britain has ever produced.
Manchester Evening Chronicle 1958

For over a decade Kenny Baker has been topping MM Polls as Britain's best trumpet player. He certainly allies a faultless technique with incredible versatility. Whether leading a section, fronting a Dixieland group, out-Calverting Eddie Calvert on a variety stage, or just playing mainstream jazz with a rhythm section, he can always be relied upon for a most musicianly job.
Melody Maker 1959

Students will listen to this virtuoso and hear power playing – throughout a phenomenal range with exciting techniques – but who needs to say anything about Kenny Baker – just buy the record and listen. Then go and practise.
The International Bandsman 1977

Kenny Baker has good reason to blow his trumpet at the age of 70. He has just been named as best trumpet of the year, and is surprised and delighted at capturing the crown worn by Humphrey Lyttleton for the past four years.
Evening Argus, Brighton 1991

The
BT British Jazz Awards
1996

THIS IS TO CERTIFY THAT

Kenny Baker's Dozen

WAS PRESENTED WITH AN AWARD
FOR WINNING THE CATEGORY OF

Big Band

ON

WEDNESDAY 1ST MAY 1996

BRITISH TELECOMMUNICATIONS PLC

BT

BBC RADIO 2 88-91 FM

And still it goes on – Kenny's latest award from the
BRITISH JAZZ AWARDS, 1996.

1	Tea For Two
2	Red Duster Rag
3	King Porter Stomp
4	Ain't Cha Got Music?
5	Stevedore Stomp
6	Ain't Misbehavin'
7	One O'Clock Jump
8	Cymbal Simon
9	Riff Up Them Stairs
10	Five Flat Flurry
11	Trunk Call
12	All Is Not Gold That Jitters
13	How Am I To Know?
14	I Wish I Were Twins
15	Soft Winds
16	Sequence
17	Needlenose
18	First Edition
19	Drop Me Off At Harlem
20	Merely A Minor
21	1-2-3-4 Jump
22	Up
23	No Script
23	Bakerloo Non-Stop

HEP records,
March 1998

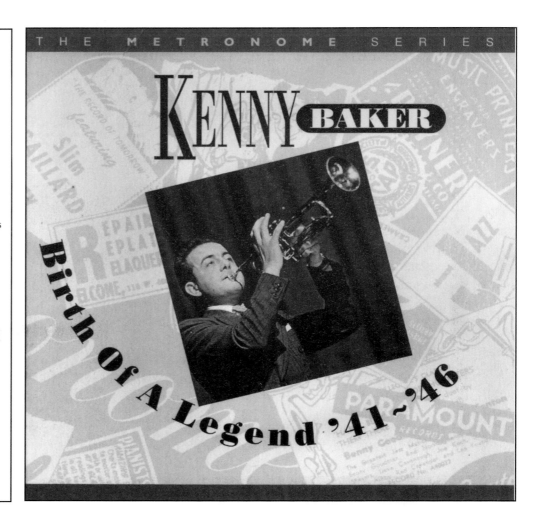

Kenny Baker plays with the drive and assurance which audiences came to expect of him, but which must have been electrifying in a 20 year old, not long down from Yorkshire.

Review of CD compilation, Birth of a Legend, '41–'46

Jazz Journal International, 1998.

THE WORLD OF RECORDINGS is changing so rapidly, that it is virtually pointless in listing LP numbers, Tape recordings or even CD sources, as companies go out of existence, amalgamate under new names, or simply delete music which they feel may not justify marketing. The positive side of this is that sometimes music is reissued under a bargain label, and the customer is happy. In these circumstances, it seems sensible to list availabilities on a web-site, and this has now been established for Kenny Baker recordings, literature and forthcoming concerts :

www.nautical.co.uk/~baker   E-mail: kenny@baker.nautical.co.uk

CHAPTER 11

WHAT NOW?

"... I retire when the phone stops ringing ..."

S O WHAT DO YOU DO when you've done it all, played everything from big band swing to bebop via trad, and have led several of the best swing bands of the day? You have also played in every conceivable venue, from Buckingham Palace to Wormwood Scrubs. Certainly life has changed in terms of seeing more of his home in Felpham near Bognor Regis. The trumpet playing continues but not via non stop travelling, and he is as likely to be playing with a youth orchestra in the Royal Albert Hall, as raising the roof with the Best of British Jazz in a venue as unusual as Chichester Cathedral. The world of professional big bands is well catered for by regular involvement with the Don Lusher Big Band, and the ever popular Ted Heath Orchestra, still going strong with the blessing of Ted's widow Moira. He also guests with the BBC Big Band, and his total radio broad-

Another birthday celebration with Sue and daughter Julie. No thoughts of retiring here!

CHELTENHAM TOWN HALL BIG BAND SPECIAL 1989 Music making can still be fun. Kenny and Don Lusher with BBC Big Band presenter Sheila Tracy.

casts must now run into many thousand hours. He still enjoys such varied fare as playing with a local group at Chichester Jazz Club or on a prestigious cruise on the newly launched luxury liner, the P&O *Oriana*.

In 1994 he was guest of honour at a celebration to commemorate the centenary of the old lighthouse in his home town of Withernsea, near Hull. The lighthouse is now part museum, with a section dedicated to his fellow star from the *Genevieve* days, Kay Kendall. They went to the same school, but never met until filming, first in *London Town*, not a great success, and then in *Genevieve*, quite the reverse.

KAY KENDALL
took lessons to master the technique of handling the trumpet for the famous nightclub scene in the 1952 film *Genevieve*. She did it so well many people believed she was actually playing! The sound was produced by a rather more accomplished player, Kenny Baker.

KENNY BAKER
and his walking partners Lucky, and Dougal.

Trumpeting a town connection

WITHERNSEA people have presented one of their most famous sons with a special plaque. Jazzman Kenny Baker was the guest of honour at the Lighthouse Centenary celebrations in Withernsea. Town Mayor Edna Harknett said the plaque marked Kenny's connections with the resort.

"It was a plaque from the people of Withernsea to Kenny who was born here and returned to the Lighthouse after many years away," she said. "The presentation was a way of commemorating his visit and it was so nice because it tied in with the centenary celebrations."

The musician who was born and spent his early years in Withernsea, played the trumpet in the film *Genevieve*, which catapulted actress Kay Kendall into worldwide fame. Kenny started his career with the Henry Chatterton band and is a renowned musician. Some of his relatives who still live in Withernsea were at the afternoon celebrations in the grounds of the Lighthouse. The event, which was arranged by the Lighthouse Trustees, was also attended by the Mayor of Holderness, Coun Ann Suggit, and civic leaders from Withernsea.

More than 150 people turned out for the occasion which helped raise money for the upkeep of a Withernsea landmark. Trustee Joy Drewery said: "We were very pleased with the

PHOTO PHIL DAWES

success of the event and delighted that Kenny came, We all enjoyed ourselves and were pleased the weather was fine.

"We held the event because Kenny came from the town and we wanted to do something to mark the 100th anniversary of the Lighthouse," she said.

SIGNAL HONOUR :
top jazz musician
Kenny Baker enjoys a
cup of tea with lighthouse
trustee Kath Jones at the
special ceremony.

HULL DAILY MAIL August 1994.

THE SOUTHERN DAILY ECHO

NAT GONELLA'S 90th BIRTHDAY PARTY
at Gosport Jazz Club — flying pants in evidence!

A special evening had the support of many of jazz's old hands, when the Gosport Jazz Club provided a party in March 1998 for the 90th birthday of Nat Gonella. It was a wild evening, with Nat insisting on entertaining the packed hall with vocals backed up by Kenny among others. The irrepressible Nat was not daunted by some of the appreciative ladies giving him the Tom Jones treatment by throwing him what appeared to be their pants!

The camper-van takes the Baker family to gigs and holidays.

It often seems as though jazz musicians either don't survive their thirties, or they go on for ever. It would be perfectly reasonable for Kenny to pack up his trumpet and concentrate on his golf, DIY, or travelling around Europe in his beloved camper van. The DIY continues apace, whether laying a substantial drive to his house, or immaculate tiling in his bathroom to a professional standard. As far as his playing is concerned, he looks at the likes of Lionel Hampton still playing at 91, Benny Carter at 92, and of course his colleagues, the mere youngsters in the Best of British Jazz. In his own words, 'I will retire when the phone stops ringing'.

His wife Sue accepts this at a time when many wives would be expecting the pipe and slippers routine to be launched. 'No chance of that, his playing is still as good as ever, and by being able to choose his gigs, we are

Kenny with wife Sue, and daughter Julie, in their garden at Felpham, Sussex.

enjoying touring the country in our camper van, really a home from home.' Daughter Julie, at present completing her degree studies at Exeter University, is quite resigned to her talented Dad still practising for hours a day. 'So many of my friends have fathers who retired at sixty five – we don't even think about it. Dad is just a ball of fire on and off the stage !'

It is a cliche to talk about 'young people of 78', but in Kenny Baker we have just that, someone who has never accepted that age has anything to do with performance. He would be the first to note any deterioration of his playing, and his top G still comes loud and clear, something that most young trumpet players would be happy to achieve. He keeps fit by a combination of Sue's great cooking and walking his two Lhasa Apso dogs.

He continues to be immensely popular with the public, and particularly with his musician colleagues. Britain has someone of whom it is justly proud, and whose contribution to the world of popular music has been immeasurable.

He is truly the Best of British.

ROBERT G. CROSBY JANUARY 1999

PHOTO COLIN BUSBY

KENNY BAKER

plays a footnote

SO MANY PEOPLE have been involved in this book, to whom I have to add my thanks, and I have to say that the whole project has given me great pleasure. Bob Crosby and I have shared many reminiscences and cups of coffee over the years, and I have always appreciated his enthusiasm and patience as the book has reached its conclusion. But most of all I feel so privileged to have been in a business where I have met so many marvellous people, far too numerous for me to mention, although many of them have appeared in these pages.

One thing is clear – if I had my time over I would do it all again.

What more could I say?